PURPOSES OF HIS HEART

*God's Plan and Purposes for
Today's Busy Woman*

Tiffany Lynn Milby

Copyright © 2009 by Tiffany Lynn Milby

Purposes Of His Heart
God's Plan and Purposes for Today's Busy Woman
by Tiffany Lynn Milby

Printed in the United States of America

ISBN 978-1-60791-895-0

All rights reserved solely by the author. The author guarantees all contents are original and do not infringe upon the legal rights of any other person or work. No part of this book may be reproduced in any form without the permission of the author. The views expressed in this book are not necessarily those of the publisher.

Unless otherwise indicated, Bible quotations are taken from The Holy Bible, New International Version®, Copyright © 1973, 1978, 1984 by International Bible Society, Used by permission of Zondervan Publishing House, and (THE MESSAGE) are taken from THE MESSAGE, Copyright © 1993, 1994, 1995, by Eugene H. Peterson, Used by permission of NavPress Publishing Group.

The front cover *heart* was designed by artist Shannon Cunningham at www.claylifestudios.com.

Contents

Acknowledgments .... *vii*

Introduction ix

Chapter 1: HIS HEART…She Would Turn Busyness into Opportunities (Not Excuses) 15
Chapter 2: HIS HEART…She Would Share Him with Others 27
Chapter 3: HIS HEART…She Would be Moved with Compassion 49
Chapter 4: HIS HEART…She Would Spend Time with Me 61
Chapter 5: HIS HEART…She Would Bless Others with Her God-given Gifts and Talents 79
Chapter 6: HIS HEART…She Would Produce Good Fruit in Her Life 95
Chapter 7: HIS HEART…She Would Influence the Next Generation for Christ 107
Chapter 8: The Struggles of HER HEART 121

Appendix A: Ideas for Using Your Spiritual Gifts and Natural Talents for Outreach 127

Appendix B: Busy Women Who Reached Out 141
Appendix C: Your Story though the Eyes of God
             (Questionnaire) 149
Appendix D: Additional Resources for Responding
             to God's Purposes 153
Notes 155
About the Author 157

Acknowledgements

First of all, thank you to my wonderful husband, Mike, for supporting me in everything I have ever desired to do in life, including writing this book. Thanks for patiently listening to all my ideas before they were ever written down. I am truly blessed to have you as my number one fan.

My kids, Austin, Alexis and Aaron, were also very supportive through this process and I thank them for that. They were very patient when Mom asked for just a few more minutes on the computer. The "A" Team also provided many outreach stories. I am very proud that my children have a heart of outreach.

Mom and Dad, thank you for being so supportive in listening to me talk about this project for almost two years! Mom, you always listened to my ideas every time I called you to share. I am blessed to have you both as such supportive parents.

My sisters, Christy and Mindy were also wonderful in reading the first manuscript and providing me feedback. You are both my *go-to* girls that I call first for everything! Not only are you my sisters, but my best friends.

Shannon, you came through with the artwork for the cover in a way that was better than I could have imagined. Thank you for allowing God to use your hands in designing the heart that summarized the whole book. It is amazing to see how God brought two little girls together over 32 years ago who both turned out to share a heart of outreach for others.

Grandma, thank you for your powerful prayers during the process of writing this book. I am very blessed to have such a strong prayer warrior covering my back!

Sherry, I am so glad I met you during the writing process. Not only are you my pastor, but you have become one of my biggest supporters. Your encouragement means more to me than you could imagine.

Thank you to all my friends who provided stories, listened to my endless talk about this project and prayed faithfully for me. I am truly blessed to have so many supportive friends.

God's Plan and Purposes for Today's Busy Woman

*But the plans of the Lord stand firm forever, the **purposes of His heart** through all generations. From heaven the Lord looks down and sees all mankind; from His dwelling place He watches all who live on earth–He who forms the hearts of all, who considers everything they do.*
Psalm 33:11, 13-15

It's an unfortunate reality that *crazy busy* has become the norm for most women in our society. It is not uncommon to hear an abrupt response of "Busy" when women are asked, "How are you doing?" We usually don't even take the time to express how we're really feeling because that would take too long! Women in particular (especially moms) fill almost every minute of their daily lives with activities. Some of us don't even realize what we are doing to ourselves until we are affected either physically or mentally. We are a stressed out and tired generation to say the least! The result of our overscheduled lives is no energy or time left for people outside our immediate family.

This is not the lifestyle God chose for us, but sadly it has become a reality for many women. God watches everything we do and hears our heart cry for more time to do the things we really want to do. He had a purpose for your life when He created you and busyness may have hindered or even stopped those plans from being fulfilled.

The good news is that it is not too late to allow God to use you to sow seeds of God's love into the lives of other busy people in your community. If you allow Him, He can use your busyness to fulfill one of the most important *purposes of His heart* which is to bless others through your life. As you intentionally allow God access to your heart, mind and soul, you will see an increase in your love for others and you will be compelled to reach out more. This is a lifelong purpose that you have to pursue and I will show you how. God's plan still stands firm through all generations which is to use His children (especially busy ones) to point searching people towards making a commitment to having a personal relationship with Jesus Christ. People are still God's most treasured creation and there are many out there who need Jesus.

Like me, you have probably come to realize that life is always changing with new seasons. It never really slows down to the pace we would like. Just when I think I'm going to slow down, another holiday sneaks up on me or it's another season of sports for one (or all) of my kids and I'm off running the busy race again. The fact is that some of us just don't have the option to become less busy. Depending on what season of life we are currently in (working a stressful job, running a household, taking care of children or aging parents), life just never seems to slow down. I also believe that some women in this generation are actually addicted to busy schedules. As soon as their obligations and commitments are fulfilled, they automatically fill that extra time with something else. Let's admit it...we are a generation that doesn't know how to say "No." To make matters worse, some women actually believe that they will appear lazy if they aren't as busy as their friends.

Over the past several years, the Lord has opened my eyes to the realization that God could use my busy life to *His* advantage and turn the craziness into outreach opportunities. God taught me this lesson just seven years ago with a life-changing event that interrupted my busy life. I will share this experience in Chapter 1. My attitude of sharing Christ with others in my life was forever changed. It became clear to me that even though I didn't realize it, my busy schedule was allowing God to *provide me with many opportunities to represent Him to others in my community*. My heart and attitude were forever changed.

Just like most people, I used my busyness as an excuse *not* to reach out and share Christ with others. As a Christian since childhood, I knew that I had a duty to share Christ's love and compassion with others but was putting this off until my kids were older. (I knew this was an excuse but just learned to live with the guilt of having this kind of attitude.) Deep down I knew that I wasn't pleasing God. While God is a patient and loving God, He isn't going to accept excuses on judgment day. When He asks us what we did for Him, I don't think the response, "I was too busy to share or care" is going to please Him. Wouldn't it be better to say to God, "I was crazy busy in this life, but I made the most of it and looked for opportunities to share you with others?"

According to Psalm 33:11, 13-15, God's purposes for us have remained the same through all generations. Although each generation has changed in its own way, God's original plan and purposes for our life never change. His ultimate plan for our lives is for us to have such a close relationship with Jesus that we (i) recognize the Holy Spirit's prompting to reach out to others, (ii) we demonstrate Him to others by being Christ-like and (iii) we use our God-given gifts and talents to draw others to Him. The way He accomplishes His plan can be done in natural ways in which we hear from God and respond by just being who God made us to be. We will explore the many ways that effective evangelism can be done as we strive to be who God designed us to be. We are to sow seeds in others that can result in their personal decision to accept Christ as their Savior. We do this by using our gifts and talents while being carriers of God's love and compassion for the world. Yet as generations have come and gone, God's original plan for our lives can seem pretty distant. In this generation, there is such competition for our attention and time that we often fail to really seek out what God's original plan and purpose was for us as Christians. Our destination as Christians is heaven, but we shouldn't stop short of living the kind of life that God had in store for us when we were created. We have the privilege of partnering with God in living a life that points others to Him. This is the way He chose to spread the good news, through the way we live our lives on this earth. Our goal should be to live a life that is focused on continuing the ministry of Jesus. To just settle for waiting for heaven is a complete loss of a surrendered life that God could have used to impact this generation. He created you with special gifts, talents, and experiences that allow you to naturally draw others to Christ through the demonstration of Christ's love and compassion to others. Jeremiah 29:11, says, "For I know the plans I have for you," declares the Lord, "plans to prosper you and not to harm you, plans to give you hope and a future." Wouldn't you love to discover why God created you to live in this generation and what His plans are for your life? I believe it is more than you have ever imagined or been willing to settle for!

    This is a handbook designed to discover the purposes of God's heart for your life. It includes getting over some barriers that keep us from reaching out, a chapter on discovering your gifts and talents and how you can use them to bless others, specific ideas for using your talents, and tools on how to build your relationship with the Lord. Most importantly, I will share how the Lord has shown me that busy Christian women literally generate the *most opportunities* to be used by God in the context of their busy lives than anyone else. Busy women really are God's secret weapon to impacting this generation for Christ! The more you are involved in various activities, the more people you meet. Just think of how many places you frequent each week (the grocery store, bank, gym, work, children's activities) and multiply that by the amount of people you come in contact with. These are all *opportunities* for God to use you to represent Him. Do you realize that *in your busyness* you can have the opportunity to *bless others* and it can be done naturally with just a little more intentionality? Don't let Satan fool you, seeds such as; offering an encouraging word, initiating a new friendship, praying for someone, cooking a meal, providing a resource book, a random act of kindness or starting a small group are powerful tools in demonstrating Christ's love with the world (and most can be done regardless of how busy you are). God uses these seeds as part of the process to bring someone into a relationship with Jesus Christ and the best way to introduce Jesus to others is by being Christ-like. When you take a genuine interest in others around you and start taking care of some of their needs, they will see Jesus. When you cultivate a heart of compassion that compels you to respond to the Lord's leading to reach out to others that you come across each day, then you can impact your community for Christ one life at a time! It's true, I have personally lived this in my own life and will share some very practical ways you can start making an impact in the lives of others immediately, despite your busy lifestyle. God loves busy women! Join me on a journey that will change the way you have perceived your busy lifestyle. Your eyes will be opened to the many opportunities that God is orchestrating in your busy day to touch another's life for Him. Let God show you the plans and purposes of His heart for your life as you read this book in the days to come. You can become a woman who impacts this generation for Christ–one life at a time!

1

HIS HEART...

She Would Turn Busyness into Opportunities (Not Excuses)

Don't shuffle along, eyes to the ground, absorbed with the things right in front of you. Look up, and be alert to what is going on around Christ—that's where the action is. See things from His perspective.
Colossians 3 (THE MESSAGE)

There is a movement across evangelical churches today which encourages Christians to share Christ's message of hope in more natural ways that replace the more confrontational methods used in the past. Remember the most common way of evangelism that encouraged people to pass out tracts to strangers while on a street corner? This method had some positive results of reaching some people but it was so uncomfortable, especially for Christians who are shy! The good news is that we have discovered methods that are effective for reaching this generation which involve more comfortable approaches such as lifestyle or servant evangelism. These evangelistic approaches are effective if people commit to take the time to nurture relationships, however this can be an overwhelming task for an already busy woman. In fact, most Christian women are aware that they need to reach out to others in their community but are often using their busy schedules as excuses. While busyness sounds like a valid excuse, it really isn't excusable.

I believe that Christian women, while realizing the importance of reaching out and sharing their faith, struggle with *guilt* because they believe they don't have enough time in their day to add one more thing. Let's face it, most woman are carrying a lot of responsibilities such as caring for their children or parents, working, managing finances, running a household, and volunteering at church or school. We are really busy. Unfortunately, we are a society that has developed several misconceptions of how evangelism is supposed to look and many have decided "it isn't for me." One of the purposes of this book is for you to discover what God's specific plan was for your life and why He created you to live in this generation. He actually designed you with specific plans in mind and equipped you with everything you would need to fulfill it. He uniquely equipped you with gifts and talents for advancing the kingdom by sharing His love and compassion with others. Despite what you have come to believe, outreach to others can become a natural part of your daily routine in the midst of your busy schedule. How outreach is demonstrated in your life may look completely different from another person's life. I have three young children, and the Lord has shown me countless ways to reach out to the people I come in contact with during the course of my busy week. It just takes the realization that your busyness can be the tool God uses in a powerful way to touch lives in your community! You are equipped, and now is the time to start using what God has already given you in order to fulfill the *purposes of His heart* for your life.

THE BUSIEST SEASON

Maybe you are like the thousands of women who have said, "One day I will slow down and have more time to do the things I really want to do." Maybe you are a mom and thought when your kids grew a little older you would have more time. I am finding that the older my kids get, the busier we are. The harsh reality is that if you don't make changes to your life now, when you finally do have more time, you'll fill your days with something else. These might include fun activities like catching up on years of scrapbooking, playing tennis, working out at the gym, decorating your home or even shopping. On the other hand, it could also be taking care of an older parent or family member. You just don't always know what life is going to throw your way. Let's face it, adding "outreach to my community" isn't going to make it to the top of your list when you do have more time. The thought of stepping out of your comfort zone and sharing Christ's love and compassion with someone else can be very intimidating. For me, reaching out to others was never at the top of my "to-do" list. I love to make lists but would never have considered adding items like "make a new friend today" or "pray for a hurting person." However, the reality is that God may bring a new friend into my life at any time, and I need to be ready and available. I also need to adjust my attitude and look for those opportunities during my busy day.

I can relate to the life of a busy woman, because I am currently a stay-at-home mom of three wonderful children– Austin, age 13, Alexis, age 10, and Aaron, age 8. I like to refer to them as the "A Team." They are all in school which allows me some free time each day with no kids home. I'm working on ways to make the most of this time, besides shopping at my favorite stores and having coffee with girlfriends every day! God has been convicting me of being a good steward of my time. Between grocery shopping three times a week because I forget items, keeping up with the never-ending laundry, cleaning the house, managing the household finances, chauffeuring kids, volunteering at school as room mom, and cooking meals that the kids complain about...my plate is more than full! Trust me, I know what it's like to be *busy*.

SOMETHING WAS MISSING

I was blessed to be raised in a Christian home. I have known since I was a child Jesus' Great Commission to share my faith with others. While I was a pretty bold little girl who would invite all her neighborhood friends to church in hopes that they would accept Jesus as their Lord and Savior, I slowly lost some of that enthusiasm as I grew up into an adult and life became a bit more complicated. I'm a tired, busy mom who realized early on that motherhood would be a bit harder than I imagined it would be. When my children were younger, I tended to be in survival mode most days. I often believed the lie Satan told me which was that I didn't have any life-changing news I could offer someone else. I barely had any brain cells left after the third baby was born (Moms, you know what I am talking about!). I had the belief that if God wanted me to share my faith with another person, they would pretty much have to *approach me* and only then would I share about the Lord. When I was in the work force, this happened on a few occasions and I was able to lead some co-workers to the Lord. I knew it was possible to share Christ without much effort on my part, but that really wasn't the type of attitude that pleased the Lord.

Even though all the busyness of motherhood was consuming my life, I had moments when I felt as if something was missing. I loved the Lord but have to admit that I didn't love *others* the way the Bible instructed me to. I often wondered if God understood my I'm-too-busy-to-share-Him attitude. After all, He is a God of grace and He should understand my situation. Maybe there was a reason for the lack of purpose and fulfillment I was experiencing? God answered this question in a very powerful way just seven years ago.

THE TRAGEDY THAT CHANGED EVERYTHING

In May of 2002, through a horrible tragedy, God showed me that it really wasn't about *me* and how *I* felt about evangelism. Earlier that year, God had placed another busy mom in my life that needed to accept Jesus as her Lord and Savior. At the time, I wasn't aware of the few days she had left on this earth nor the impact I would have on her eternal destiny. God interrupted my busy life with an event that would change my Christian walk forever. As a result, my opinion about outreach to unbelievers, especially to other busy women, was forever changed. I realized for the first time that I could not use the excuse of waiting until my kids were older to share Christ's love and compassion with the world. God had significant plans to use me in the midst of my busy schedule in the life of a friend who needed a Savior almost immediately.

In 1998, we moved to the city of Placentia in Southern California. It was the perfect city to live in with a lot of young families and plenty of activities for my children. I joined the Placentia MOMS Club® shortly after we moved into the community with the goal of meeting new friends with kids. The MOMS Club® is a non-profit city club for stay-at-home moms. It was the perfect opportunity to meet other moms and kids in our area. Not long after I joined, I was voted the new president. I tend to jump right into things and thought, president...hey, why not! A few months after becoming president, I started a weekly neighborhood Bible study group with some of my Christian friends from the MOMS Club®. The thought of having real conversations with other moms without interruptions a few hours a week sounded like fun! I have to admit that I wasn't very spiritual in praying about starting the group and didn't consider whether God was leading me to start it; I just did it. One of my gifts is administration, so starting a group was easy for me to do. In the beginning, I never could have guessed our group's potential of becoming an outreach to moms in the community who were searching for something more. God had plans to use this group in a way that I never could have imagined. It really was His idea.

I will never forget the month that Kim starting coming to the Moms Christian Fellowship I started with my friends. At one of the first meetings she attended we had just learned that a mom in the community, whom many of us knew, had lost her husband and three young children in a house fire. I still remember the room full of grieving moms sitting in disbelief and trying to figure out how something like this could have possibly happened. We tried to comfort each other and made comments like, "something good has got to come out of this." We had no idea how to process this tragedy. We were really stunned and not sure how to comfort each other. Kim eventually spoke up in tears and said, "I may be new at all this, but how could something good come out of a woman losing her husband and children?" We came to the quick realization that there are some tragedies that simply can't be explained.

On most Wednesdays, Kim would sit quietly and listen to the group discuss different biblical studies. She seemed to be absorbing the Bible teachings we were sharing about and the testimonies of what the Lord was doing in each other's lives. One day she opened up and shared at the end of the meeting. Kim expressed a growing faith which started when the Lord answered several of her prayers. The other moms were so excited to see Kim's new faith and believed the group was making an actual difference in her life. Unfortunately, our excitement soon turned into grief.

Almost three weeks after she shared, Kim and her husband went on a trip out of town to help a friend who was in the process of divorcing her abusive husband. Kim and her husband were thoughtful friends and went to help her with some things around the house. In the early morning hours, their friend's estranged husband broke into the house while they were still asleep and shot both Kim and her husband to death. This man had every intention of killing everyone in the house that day. In fact, he had held the gun to his wife's head, but it jammed and her life was spared. He then walked out of the house, sat down on the driveway and called 911 to turn himself in. Thankfully, Kim's daughter was staying with her grandmother and wasn't in the house. Kim's stepson was not harmed even though he was sleeping in another room in the house when the incident occurred. In fact, the house was full of kids who slept through the whole ordeal. God protected those children.

I can still remember the morning that I walked into the club meeting and heard the terrible news about my friend. The worst thing a mother could have imagined just happened to my friend. She left her three-year-old daughter an orphan. Her stepson lost his father. How could this have happened? I remember telling my husband that I would never be the same. I felt such fear come over me that something could happen to my family next. It was overwhelming. First a mom in my community lost her family in a fire, and now another friend lost her life in a violent act. These were within a few months of each other, and both incidents a mother's worst nightmare. However, in the midst of my fears and disbelief, God comforted and reminded me of the testimony Kim shared at the last Bible study meeting she attended. She acknowledged the Lord was working in her life and she professed her new faith in Him. Suddenly, I realized she was placed in our group to prepare her for eternity! I began to think, What if I had been too caught up in my own busy life and never started this group? What if the other moms had never invited her to our group? What if the friend that gave her a ride each week to make it easier for her to attend had never offered? I was overwhelmed by the reality that this social Bible study group was crucial in the process of bringing another mom into a relationship with the Lord just weeks before her death. God used me in the midst of my busyness to start this group that saved another woman's life for eternity. What I thought was my idea, turned out to be a part of God's plan and purpose for my life.

It is His desire to use people to impact a life for Him. Are you willing to become available to the purposes of His heart for your life? There may be someone in your life who has a limited amount of time left on this earth and you may be the one God desires to use to change that life forever.

THE MOST OPPORTUNITIES

Satan would love that busy women everywhere believe the lie that they don't have enough time to incorporate outreach that shares Christ's love and compassion with the world. He wants nothing more than for you to stay so busy with your schedule that you miss out on the very divine appointments that God is placing in your life right now. Errands are run with one eye on the clock and the other on the to-do list, with zero consideration given to the needs of the clerk standing at the checkout or the person filling the prescription.[1] Sadly, it is also not uncommon for Christians to become so busy with church activities that they miss out on opportunities to share Christ with the rest of the world. If you are waiting until you have enough time it is too late! I am here to let you know as one busy woman to another—*now,* during the busiest season of your life, you have the *most opportunities* to impact another person's life. I know it doesn't make sense and this is not what the world tells you, but it's absolutely true. Just think about the many people you come in contact with each week, whether it is through work, your child's school activities, involvement in sports, clubs, the gym, or other activities you are involved in on a regular basis. When you aren't busy, you don't come in contact with as many people. These are opportunities to meet and reach out to people you may not normally come in contact with later in life. For moms, you will most likely make lifelong friends from the relationships you establish now. There will be people that God brings into this busy time of your life that He desires you to touch. Whether it is through a friendship for a season or a lifetime, it is God's heart to use you now.

Many people I reach out to have attended a church at some point in life but left in their college or young adult years when the decision became their own. On the other hand, there are some people who were forced to go to church as children, but despite their knowledge, they never made a personal decision to pursue a relationship with Jesus Christ. I have found that the majority of people you establish a relationship with are open to an invitation to your church if you just ask them. Most women especially love invitations to attend women's ministry events such as a fashion show, tea or brunch. You would be surprised at how many women are out there just waiting for someone like you to step out and offer the hand of friendship. Moms of young children are a group that especially needs friends and encouragement. You can be the one who shares with them that they can trust their children's safety and well-being to the Lord, and they can draw strength to get through the hardest of days out of a relationship with Jesus. Moms can live with a lot of fears regarding the safety and well-being of their children. As Christians, we have the answers and encouragement the world is searching for. We carry the good news of Christ's sovereignty and control over the lives of His children and we should share it with the world! Every person on earth needs to hear this.

It is God's desire that you partner with Him and make an investment in the lives of people in your community. He is already actively working in those around you. Please join Him on a daily basis. The next time you see a neighbor, think about why God put you both on the same street. Was there a specific reason? When you attend the next soccer practice, ask God if there are any moms He wants you to befriend. The next time you go to the grocery store, consider if God wants you to encourage the clerk. See everything you do with God's perspective. Ask Him how He desires you to reach out into the lives of others that come along your path.

Women, there is an urgency to reach out and you cannot afford to wait until you are less busy. As time goes by, you may become even busier. It may be years before you have time, and by then you will have missed thousands of opportunities to impact lives in your community now. In fact, you may have a "Kim" in your life right now whose days on earth are few.

Throughout this book, I will share what the Lord has shown me in the area of incorporating outreach into a busy woman's lifestyle. When we reach out by using our gifts and talents, it becomes natural and fulfilling. A busy woman living with God's purpose in mind can incorporate outreach as a lifestyle, not just an event. A busy woman has the potential to powerfully impact her community for Christ–one life at a time! You will learn in this book that you are the tool that God wants to use in reaching a lost and confused world! Join me on a journey to find out how God designed you uniquely and how easily outreach can become a part of whom you are. It doesn't have to be uncomfortable when you are just being who God designed you to be with the purposes of His heart in mind!

OUR HEART'S RESPONSE

Read Ezekiel 11:19

1. What type of heart do you have towards others in your community?

    a. If you feel like your heart has been hardened, begin praying for "a heart of flesh" today.

2. What are your specific excuses or hindrances for not reaching out to others?

3. Does the idea of reaching out to others make you uncomfortable? If so, why?

4. What have been your previous experiences in reaching out?

5. In an average week, how many people do you think you come in contact with?

    a. List three people you can take steps to cultivate a friendship with this year.
    b. Pray that God will help you to see the divine appointments He has scheduled for you.

2

HIS HEART...

She Would Share Him with Others

Do you not say, "Four months more and then the harvest?" I tell you, open your eyes and look at the fields! They are ripe for harvest.
John 4:35

I love the way that Steve Sjogren describes how most Christians really feel about evangelism in his book *Conspiracy of Kindness*. He writes, "For most Christians doing evangelism is a lot like going to the dentist; no one really enjoys doing it, but it has to be done every once in a while." Do these words ring true for you? They did for me. I was like most Christians who associated evangelism with an uncomfortable task I was obligated to do once in a while (I admit that I experienced guilt when too much time passed since I gave out my last Bible tract). It's very common for most Christians to have misconceptions about evangelism and the way they should do it. Some have the opinion that evangelism is done only at church-planned outreaches or an event like handing out tracts on the street corner. There is a major difference between doing evangelism and living a lifestyle that incorporates outreach into every area of your life. Let's examine this idea further and see how to live it out in your own busy day.

BUSY WOMEN PARTNERING WITH GOD = GENERATION IMPACT!

As I have matured in my faith over the years, God has shown me that if I truly desire to live a life that impacts others then I must become available to listen to His leading and not be afraid to act on what He is asking me to do. This requires me to slow down and be aware of my surroundings, which can be hard for a busy woman! After all, Jesus is a perfect gentleman and although He desires to use me in sharing His love with people, it is still *my* choice (and I can still say "No"). I have to admit that there have been times that He led me to reach out to someone and I didn't do it because my *what ifs* got in the way. I work hard to not let fear get in the way of what God directs me to do, because outreach can be uncomfortable at times. I love the Lord dearly and want to give Him my life to be used as He pleases. Besides, I don't like that regretful feeling of knowing that I just blew it by not being responsive to the Lord. The good news is that the Lord is patient and will give us many more chances even when we feel like we have blown it.

I believe that opportunities for outreach start with a desire and the desire starts when you spend time with Jesus (more on this in Chapter 4). I once had a strong desire to muster up enough courage to offer to pray for a stranger during my busy day. (This was unusual so it had to be the Lord!) Now let me tell you where that desire landed me! I was at the beach one summer day with my kids when I noticed an elderly woman sitting on the beach with a boogie board next to her. It was one of those, what's-wrong-with-this-picture-moments and I blurted out, "You didn't go in that cold water did you?" In California, the water can be very cold and that day it was freezing! She said "Oh yes." This started a conversation and she began to share with me that she had hurt her back, was supposed to be on bed rest but thought that the cold water might do her back some good! She told her husband she was going to the store and went to the beach instead! I instantly felt in my spirit that this was the woman I was supposed to pray for. It turned out she was a Christian, so my offer to pray for her back was well received. I laid hands on her right there on the beach and prayed that the Lord would heal her. When I was done she said, "I had just prayed this week that the Lord would send someone to pray for me and here you are!" God had brought us together that day on the beach. I never saw her again, but I believe God healed her back that day. And what a great story! It also built up my faith to step out more in praying for others. I recently offered to pray for the director of a reading clinic my youngest son was attending after she shared with me that she was going to be taking a leave of absence to have heart surgery. I admit, I had to get over my fears before I asked her. I think I even stuttered to get the words out when offering to pray for her! My kids were with me and after class we all stepped outside and laid hands on her to pray for God's healing of her heart condition. When we left I asked my kids what they thought about what we had just done and my youngest said, "We're Christians. That's what we always do." I had forgotten some of the other times we had stepped out as a family and prayed for a stranger, but he had not. I love it when I get those moments to minister in the community with my kids.

Just think about how many times a stranger has told you personally about all their ailments. Maybe you were like me and thought why are you telling me all this? Have you ever thought that maybe there was a purpose to someone opening up to you? In fact, these can be a signal that the door is open to an opportunity to minister to their specific need. God might want you to offer to pray for them, offer an encouraging word or even offer to take care of a physical need. Let me tell you what happened to me one day. During the course of writing this book I was faced with an opportunity for ministry at the nail salon. I was getting my nails done one day when out of the blue the technician said, "Ouch, my leg!" I asked her what was wrong and she told me that she didn't know, but that it had been hurting for a while. She then began to tell me that her husband had been out of work for six months and that she didn't have the money to go to the doctor. They did not have medical insurance and her concern of not being able to work showed in her face. I felt the Holy Spirit's prompting to offer to pray for her pain. I said something like this, "I believe in Jesus and have prayed for many people whom He has healed. The Bible says that if you have even just a little bit of faith, God can heal you. If you agree with me that you have faith that God can heal your leg, I would love to pray for you." Her eyes were so big and appeared to be fighting back tears. It was as if she was so shocked she couldn't even speak. She shook her head, but I couldn't tell if it was a yes or no response. So I continued and said to her, "I know you are at work, but if you give me permission to pray for you, it's okay to keep your eyes open." She shook her head yes. As I prayed for her, I bowed my head because it was a little awkward looking straight at her with our eyes open. (I'm not used to someone staring at me!) When we were done, I asked her how she felt. She stood up and said, "It doesn't hurt!" When she was done with my nails, she gave me a hug and I left. I noticed that evening that my nail didn't look right and I needed to go back in the next day to have it fixed. I was a little hesitant because I wondered how she would act towards me. As soon as I walked in, she ran up and gave me a hug and said her leg was still better! She then began to tell me that the owner's wife was in the hospital and could I say a prayer for her. Another technician came up to us, then another. A lady getting a pedicure yelled, "Are you having a party over there?" The next thing I know one of the technicians is telling me she has been having stomach pain for two weeks and just went in for an ultrasound the day before. I asked, "Do you want me to pray for you?" She said, "Yes!" We stepped outside and I told her that she needed to have faith that God could heal her. She said, "Oh yes I believe in God, Jesus and Buddha!" I said "Okay" and prayed for her. I know that one day I will be able to share the Gospel with these ladies, but for now God is using me to demonstrate His healing power and I don't think there is a better way to introduce them to my Jesus!

Women like to talk and can sometimes open up at the most unexpected times, especially if they are going through trials. Next time someone shares with you, offer to pray for them on the spot versus telling them, "I'll be praying for you." It has a much bigger impact and takes more risk on our part, but God *loves* risk takers and will often show up in a powerful way when you step out in faith. Can you recall some Bible heroes who stepped out in faith? David stepped out and fought a giant with a slingshot…that was a *risk*! How about Daniel? He prayed to God even though he knew he could be punished for going against the law. He took a risk and prayed anyway. When he was thrown into the lions' den and left to die, God showed up and protected him. God responds to risk takers! When you take a risk to pray for someone on the spot it allows God the opportunity to demonstrate His power that changes lives. Step out in faith next time someone you meet opens up and shares something personal. It may be a green light for a divine appointment.

MISCONCEPTIONS OF OUTREACH

There is a widespread misconception among many Christians who believe that their faith should be kept private and only shared on special occasions when someone actually asks questions. Keeping your belief in Jesus private was never one of God's ideas. It is actually a lie that Satan has fabricated. In fact it goes against the ultimate plan of God using His own children to point others to Him. In Matthew 28:19-20, Jesus gives *the Great Commission* to "go and make disciples of all nations." This seemingly difficult commission ends with the comforting words "and surely I am with you always." We are not given this commission to venture out on our own efforts alone. It is a *partnership* with Christ. If we allow Him, He will use our words, hands and sometimes finances to move a person closer to making a decision to follow Christ. If He doesn't use *us*, then who else will He use? Jesus came to this earth 2,000 years ago and demonstrated to us what a life of servanthood must look like. He was very effective in His compassion ministry and it still serves as a perfect example of how we can live a life of outreach. As Christians, we can easily miss the message that it is God's desire to use everyday people to continue the ministry of Jesus on earth. This is done through living a lifestyle that is always watching and waiting for God's direction to engage in what He is doing in the lives of others around us. We leave the results of our efforts to God. We simply live a life that responds to what He is telling us to do in the moment.

Another misconception about outreach is that you have to possess the gift of evangelism in order to reach out to unbelievers. Every single Christian is called to share Christ's love and salvation message with the world. It doesn't matter who you are. We are all equipped and expected to play a role in pointing people to our Savior Jesus Christ. Mark 16:15 says,

"He [Jesus] said to them, Go into all the world and preach the good news to all creation." He didn't say, all those who feel qualified go and share the good news, because nobody would go! My guess is that none of us feel qualified enough to make a difference; that is why we need the Holy Spirit's power and guidance.

It's true that some Christians are gifted as evangelists and it's more natural for them to reach out to others. In Ephesians 4:12, God reveals to us that those with the gift of evangelism are to "prepare God's people for works of service so that the body of Christ may be built up." This means that it is the evangelist's responsibility to help the body of Christ *catch the vision* of outreach thus equipping them. It is *not* the sole responsibility of the evangelist to save this generation. Don't be fooled, you have no excuse even if you don't feel gifted when it comes to evangelism. If you have a personal relationship with Jesus Christ, then God can use you!

Despite what many have come to believe, outreach can blend into every part of our lives. It doesn't have to be compartmentalized or performed only on special occasions. It shouldn't be another event scheduled into your calendar (like taking the dog to the groomer). For example, I can remember as a teenager going to the beach to hand out tracts on the street corner. It was actually fun handing them out with a group of friends and doing evangelism together. I never really felt successful at it because I never saved anyone, but I did get several phone numbers from cute boys! I have to admit after one evening of passing out tracts, I did have a sense of accomplishment that I could check off evangelism as *done* for the year.

Again, effective evangelism isn't supposed to be something that you checked off your calendar as *done* or measured by how many people got saved. Most often than not, God will use you to sow seeds into the life of someone He is already in the process of drawing to Him. Your part in drawing someone closer to accepting Jesus as Savior may be as simple as buying them a Christian book on an area they are struggling with. You can learn to do what God asks you to do in the moment if you slow down to listen and become available. More often than not, it will be small acts done with intentionality and thought that have the greatest impact. Outreach doesn't have to be awkward or scary. When someone prays to accept the Lord, it isn't because of your persuasive words, but rather the Holy Spirit has been at work in that person's life for some time. It doesn't happen very often that a person hears the gospel for the first time and then immediately prays to receive the Lord. It can be a long process that you can be a part of when you respond to the Lord's direction to share Christ's love. You can have the privilege of being a part of that process no matter how big or small a part you play.

Remember that effective evangelism is not limited to just sharing the message of the gospel. Outreach done Jesus' style is more natural and touches lives in many different ways. Jesus didn't wait for people to come to Him; He ministered along His way in many different ways. He will guide you in each situation He brings along your path as you stay closely connected to Him. There will be many opportunities along your own way in life to minster to others like Jesus did.

AUTHENTIC CHRISTIANS

There is a real need for Christians to be authentic (faults and all) with people they meet, especially around unbelievers. Unfortunately there are a lot of Christians who appear almost *too perfect* to the rest of the world. They are afraid to talk about what is really going on in their lives for fear of being judged they don't have it all together. This does a disservice to non-Christians by misleading them into believing they have to be cleaned up before they can come to Christ. The other problem is that they may feel like they can't relate to those perfect Christians. The truth is, Christians struggle with the same issues as the rest of the world including depression, infidelity, financial difficulties, and serious illness. However, the difference between Christians and the world is that we know God is with us and we can draw on His strength to get us through the toughest circumstances. This supernatural strength helps us get through life when things are not easy. Another difference between Christians and unbelievers is how they handle pain; that can become the biggest testimony of a faith worth having. Sometimes pain is the one thing that brings us and others closer to the Lord. Don't be deceived into believing that how you live your life when things are challenging or even devastating doesn't have an impact on your unsaved friends. Dwight L. Moody put it this way, "Of one hundred men, one will read the Bible; the ninety-nine will read the Christian." Your life and actions have a greater impact on others than you can possibly imagine.

Let me tell you about my friend, Gina whose life was a great witness to both Christians and unbelievers. She was a young mother of three children who attended the same public elementary school as my children. My daughter has gone to school with her youngest son since preschool. Shortly after Gina's youngest child was born, she was diagnosed with cancer. She was only 32 years old. The type of cancer she had was slow growing but very painful. It did not respond to chemotherapy, so there was nothing they could do but wait. The rare cancer would attack her nerves causing her to experience excruciating pain. Gina had tumors throughout her body and towards the end of her life walked with a cane because of severe leg pain. She was on a number of strong medications to help manage her pain. Her husband said she would wake up at 4:30 a.m. every morning just to take her pain medications so that they would start working before her children woke up for school. When the pain was manageable, Gina would make her kids a nutritious breakfast and get them off to school. Her family was her biggest priority and everyone knew that. Regardless of how bad she felt, she would make every effort to personally pick her children up from school each day, standing there to greet them with a smile. She met them face to face on the schoolyard until two weeks before she lost her battle with the cancer. After Gina passed away her husband allowed me to borrow her Bible for a special memorial for all the moms who knew her at the school. I came across some Bible study notes that Gina had made on the subject of pain folded neatly in her Bible. She wrote, "Pain from the hand of God can be trusted. He always means it for good in our lives because we know He is faithful to always want the best for us. We need to remember that it is better to walk with Christ and be in pain, than to turn from Him and be happy." This mom was acquainted with suffering in a way most of us will never comprehend, yet she had peace in the midst of her circumstances. The world is looking for the kind of peace that allowed Gina to be so strong and brave for her children, which truly was a gift from the Lord. Gina's life was a testimony to the people at school who saw her put her kids first each day and meet them with a smile regardless of how much pain she was feeling. She was known as a strong woman of God in our community who was actively living out her faith and trust in the Lord. She was one of the strongest Christian women I knew and her life was a great testimony. Everyone who heard her story was amazed. I know that her life was used to lead many people toward the sovereignty of the Lord. She always said that she wanted her cancer to count and it did. It was a blessing to know her.

Don't be afraid to talk freely about what is going on in your own life, struggles and all. When my friend Gina was sick, I spoke about her often with others. Her story was a true testimony of Christ's strength and peace in the midst of difficult circumstance. Realize that lives can be impacted as you share your own struggles or those of others you know. Share specific ways that God has answered you or your friend's prayers. This shows others that you serve a God who listens and cares enough to supernaturally answer prayer. Non-Christians (neighbors, co-workers, friends and more) are watching your lifestyle to see if what you have is something they are missing. Don't underestimate the power of your example. When people don't know Christ, they are deciding if what Christians have is relevant and the missing piece in their lives. Many people allow busyness to fill the empty ache in their hearts. Sometimes when people are busy enough the ache in their heart can be ignored for a season. Christians can also do this and neglect to grow deeper in their walk with the Lord. Busyness is a temporary fix to the emptiness people can experience. Christ is the only one who can permanently fill us up with contentment. Jesus said in Luke 19:10, "For the son of man came to seek and save what was lost." Follow His example. Find those lost people in your community and direct them to Christ. You have the missing piece to their life!

ACTIONS SPEAK THE LOUDEST

As I said before, how we live as Christians impacts the lives around us in a significant way. For a mother, not only does she have the opportunity to raise her own children to love the Lord, but when she shares her faith with another person, her children are taught a valuable lesson. Reaching out to others is a great example for children to learn about sharing Christ's love when they see their mother putting her own faith into action. They are taught what it looks like to put into practice what they have been taught at home and at Sunday school. In other words, they learn what it means to walk the talk. I had a great experience that taught my kids this very lesson. I was once approached by a young man outside the exit door of a store. He was standing there asking each person as they went by for money to buy food. I told him that I would be willing to buy him dinner at the restaurant inside the store. He agreed and followed us in and I bought him dinner. I didn't even realize the impact that this act of kindness would have on my children until my youngest son, Aaron, brought it up almost six months later. He said out of the blue one day, "That was really nice of you, Mommy, when you buyed that guy dinner." He had learned a valuable lesson by watching his mom demonstrate Christ's compassion to a hungry person. It is your job as a mother to teach your children this. The concept of putting others first is a value that the world doesn't teach, so it is our responsibility as mothers to demonstrate how this is done for our children. They learn about serving others most often from their family and church related activities. The world has the "all about me" mentality and "what will I get out of this?" That isn't how we want our next generation to live and treat others. It is the total opposite of how the Bible teaches us to live. If we are not careful, our kids will develop this type of attitude by what they are watching on television. I monitor what programs my kids are allowed to watch for this very reason.

Women, isn't it comforting to know that there is more to life than crazy busy schedules? When we have the hardest of days, we can still crawl up into the lap of Jesus and He refills our soul. The hope of one day meeting face to face with our Savior and Lord Jesus Christ can melt away the cares of the world, because we know our stress is only temporary. If you are at all like me, I am sure there are days when you can't wait to get to heaven (of course you don't want to literally die, but a mansion that you don't have to clean sounds pretty nice!). As Christians, we have a hope of spending eternity in God's presence, walking the streets of gold, feeling no more pain, and reuniting with loved ones. The hope for eternity should not stop us from living out our life now on this earth and should compel us to share Christ with the world so they can experience the same. There are millions of good people that will be going to hell if they don't accept Jesus as their Lord and Savior. If we don't take the time to engage in the ministry of Jesus and reach out to those people, then who will? 1 John 3:18 says, "let us not love with words or tongue but with actions and in truth." Jesus commands us to have a faith that is *active*. He desires a faith that reaches out to others in both action and words; to do anything less in my opinion is letting God down. *Because* we are Christians we have the tremendous opportunity to give thanks to God for what He did for us on the cross and live a life that is trying to take as many people as we can to heaven with us.

Know that your acts of kindness done in Jesus' name does impact people more than you know. It may actually help them in their search for something more and move them closer to ultimately accepting Him as their Lord and Savior. He desires that you share His love and compassion with others, and this can be done as easily as offering an ear to listen to a person who is having a bad day. You are demonstrating Christ's love and compassion by listening and offering encouragement. Slow down and be attentive to the Holy Spirit's leading, He will show you creative ways to reach out in many different situations.

HOW CAN YOU USE ME TODAY?

The first step to live a life of being available to God is to *slow down* and listen to God's quiet whisper of instruction. As you wait in line, shop, sit at the soccer field or even work; ask God, *"How can you use me today?"* There is a good chance that you will need to take steps to quiet your surroundings in order to hear His response. Maybe the next time you drive in the car you turn your radio off so you can pray and listen to Him. Listening to the Holy Spirit is key to effective outreach. Sometimes God's response to our question is in a thought or idea that you know isn't your own. Don't question it–just do what He asks you to do. On some occasions, you may feel led to reach out to someone but not know what to say or do. Try to start a conversation and see if God gives you anything. I know this sounds really awkward, but I have a friend who when she isn't sure exactly what to say, often tells people that God loves them. Saying this starts a conversation in many situations and the person ends up opening up to her. She can then listen to what the Lord is directing her to do next and many times she has an opportunity to share Christ. Remember when we take a risk, it invites God to show up in ways we didn't plan or imagine.

As believers, we are the vessels that bring Jesus' love into the lives of unbelievers. It is the way God chooses to demonstrate His love and compassion to the world and we get to be in on it! 2 Corinthians 3:3 says, "You show that you are a letter from Christ, the result of our ministry, written not with ink but with the Spirit of the living God, not on tablets of stone but on tablets of human hearts." We are God's love letter to the world. What does your letter look like? Is it clear who you belong to? Would people be able to recognize you as a follower of Christ or do you blend in with the rest of the world? You are a representation of who Christ is. We should emanate His nature. It is both a responsibility and tremendous opportunity to engage in His compassion ministry to the world. We are to communicate His love to the lives of people everywhere. God may use you daily, weekly, or once in a while. The important thing is to not be so caught up in your day-to-day routines that you miss out on the special opportunities that Christ has planned as part of your day.

RELATIONSHIP IS KEY

Every person has a group of people they come in contact with weekly. Intentionally recognize opportunities to reach out. In my life, I go through seasons with my friendships. I might see the same families for a whole soccer season and that is my time to sow seeds in their lives. After soccer season, I may not see those moms as often. We are all so busy it is easy to be friends with the ones we see on a weekly or daily basis. Just be aware that in every season, you will most likely have several harvest fields (work, school, the gym, your child's sport activities, etc.) to cultivate relationships and look for opportunities for God to use you. You may also have opportunities in the most unlikely places. I once traveled on a plane to visit my sister and had an opportunity to reach out to a woman during a flight. I had noticed her in the line at the airport while we waited to board. Once we boarded and I found my seat, she ended up sitting right across the aisle from me. She noticed that the book I was carrying was a Christian book my Bible study group was reading and we started talking. She said some ladies at her church had told her about the same book and suggested she buy a copy. I shared with her about the book and we talked for the rest of the flight. I did sense that the Lord was doing something in her life, but wasn't sure how He wanted to use me that day. I also noticed that she was wearing a brace on her wrist and thought maybe God wanted me to offer to pray for her. I asked her what was wrong and she told me. I kept thinking that I should offer to pray for her wrist, but just didn't have a peace about it. As we walked off the plane and headed for the exit, I was still struggling with what God wanted me to do since I knew it wasn't a mistake that we had connected on the plane. At the last minute before we said good bye, I felt impressed to give her the book. She was so touched and couldn't believe that I would do such a nice thing. Even though I didn't offer to pray for her, I did what God wanted me to do in the moment. God used me as a resource provider to assist her in her spiritual walk. You too, have the potential to touch a random life during your busy day. Don't underestimate what a simple act of kindness such as giving a stranger a book can do for their soul.

    When I first meet people, I try not to tell them that I am a Christian right away. In fact, my pastor recently recommended to us that when asked what we believe, to say, "I'm a follower of Jesus." I'm going to start saying that from now on, because sometimes when people hear "Christian" they have negative opinions associated with that term. Over time I may talk about answered prayers, my church or Bible study, but I want my life to speak louder than words. I am a passionate follower of Jesus Christ and I want that to be a reflection of everything I do. I know that being Christ-like is the best way to introduce people to my Jesus. Also, Christians who use a lot of *Christianese* can really be a turn off to unbelievers. When we say things like "God bless you," "the Lord's will," "have faith," or "just believe," people really don't have any idea what we are talking about. You shouldn't have to announce to the world that you are a Christian. Let your life demonstrate who you are in Christ by your actions. Trust me, people will notice what you are all about without you even telling them. From experience, I have discovered that when I start talking about my faith right away, I am suddenly avoided (they probably think that I'm going to try and save them). However, when I try to live my life like Jesus did, which is a daily effort on my part, people notice a difference and stick around. It has been interesting to see how many people feel the urge to go back to church just from hanging around other Christians. That is the power of the Holy Spirit at work in and through us. God will show you the right words and timing to share the gospel, but let your actions peak their interest first.

Genuine compassion which compels us to do acts of kindness will have the greatest results in breaking down the walls to people's hearts. These acts open the door to other people receiving our friendship. When we do something unexpected for someone, they are touched deeply. There are a lot of people who have experienced painful situations and relationships. This may cause them to be more hesitant to receive an act of kindness or accept your offer to help, but don't give up! As you continue to show them that you are genuinely concerned about them, the walls to their heart will slowly begin to crumble. An important point is to reach out with no hidden agenda of being friends just so you can save them. I guarantee that if you develop friendships with people who are different than you, one day you will have an opportunity to share about Jesus with them. Also, don't be friends only with people who are exactly like you, or only Christians. This is a very easy trap to fall into. If you don't have any non-Christian friends, go out and find some! They are everywhere if you just look around.

THE SOWING TEAM

Christ does not give you the burden of saving every person in your life, but rather asks you to be available to respond when He leads (however that may look). We can each play a role in directing someone towards Christ. What role each one of us plays is up to Christ. We are to sow seeds wherever we go, leaving the results of their growth to God. When we develop relationships and show people compassion through acts of kindness, we have a great opportunity to point them toward Christ.

It is important to realize that you are part of a sowing team. It is easy to get caught up in the pressure to close the deal and lead someone in the Sinner's Prayer. We tend to measure success by whether or not they said *the prayer*!

I know, I have put this pressure on myself many times. However, this is *not* a pressure that the Lord has put on us, we place it on ourselves. God has *not* told me that I must save a certain number of people a month or else. Instead, He has impressed upon me that I should always be looking for opportunities to be used in His name. We are His *hands here on earth*. I once heard it said this way, "Christ has no body now on earth but yours, no hands but yours, no feet but yours; yours are the eyes through which Christ's compassion looks out on the world, yours are the feet with which He is to go about doing good and yours are the hands with which He is to bless us now."[2] If we see a need and don't do anything to help, how will that further the kingdom or bring glory to God? In Romans 10 of The Message Bible it says, "Everyone who calls, 'Help, God!' gets help. But how can people call for help if they don't know who to trust? And how can they know who to trust if they haven't heard of the One who can be trusted? And how can they hear if nobody tells them? And how is anyone going to tell them, unless someone is sent to do it?" We are the ones who God desires to send to touch lives to introduce Him to the world! The Bible says in 1 Corinthians 3:9, that *"we are God's co-workers."*

2 Corinthians 9:6, says, "Whoever sows sparingly will also reap sparingly, and whoever sows generously will also reap generously." While I have sown many seeds, I have personally only had a handful of opportunities to pray the Sinners Prayer with someone who was ready. I'm okay with that because I realize that the pressure is not on me to save them, I am co-working with what God has already been doing in their lives. I am playing the role that God ordained for me in their life. In fact, God may choose to use a whole team of sowers to work in the life of a unbeliever for years until the day he or she finally accepts the Lord. My grandfather accepted the Lord just weeks before he died of leukemia. I had prayed for him for years as a child and saw my prayer

answered just weeks before his death. It's important to realize that most people come to know the Lord not through an event but through a family member, co-worker, or friend. A friend of my great-grandmother was the one who led my grandfather to the Lord. Personal interaction and going through life together is the key to sowing seeds. You may or may not have the privilege of seeing the results of the seeds you are sowing in this lifetime. If you do step out and share the gospel and it is rejected don't take it personally. They are really rejecting Jesus. I believe when you arrive in heaven, God will show you the results of your being available to sow seeds for Him and the fruits of your labor.

JUST ONE WOMAN

One evening during my quiet time, I had an amazing revelation from the Lord that ignited both a passion and a burden to reach out to people already a part of my life. Let me explain. As I was reading my Bible one night, all the verses on the goodness of the Lord seemed to jump off the pages and I suddenly felt an overwhelming response of despair for unbelievers in this world. I felt such a personal responsibility to share Christ with others mixed with an emotion of helplessness. I literally felt that the idea of God desiring to use me to share Him with others was too overwhelming and I couldn't possibly make a difference. I also felt paralyzed to even try. I know it can be intimidating to share Jesus with others and the natural response is to think we can't do it and leave the job to the Billy Grahams of this world. Something happened in the midst of my overwhelming emotions. God revealed to me that there were certain people He had placed in my life whom I could impact one-on-one *now*. Most of these people would never attend a Billy Graham crusade but would accept an invitation to church or a Bible study if I just asked.

My worst nightmare would be to get to heaven one day and have Jesus show me the faces of all the people who came across my path that He wanted me to reach out to, but I didn't, because I was too busy. I urge you to make a decision today to allow God to use you to reach out to others while there is still time. Our time on this earth can be very short. I did not know that my friend Kim had a limited amount of days left on this earth when He brought her into my life. If I had not reached out to her, I would have had major regrets.

Let your prayer be that of Bill Hybels in *Just Walk Across the Room*[1]: "My life is in your hands, God. Use me to point someone toward you today—I promise to cooperate in any way I can. If you want me to say a word for you today, I'll do that. If you want me to keep quiet but demonstrate love and servanthood, by your Spirit's power I will. I'm fully available to you today, so guide me by your Spirit."

OUR HEART'S RESPONSE

Read Luke 19:10

1. What does this verse say that Jesus came to do?

    a. Are you following His example in searching for the lost?
    b. Do you have many non-Christians in your life? If not, what steps can you take to meet more people?

2. Has God answered any of your specific prayers that you can share as encouragement with others?

3. How does your life look different from an unbeliever?

4. What are some of the excuses that have kept you from reaching out to others (besides your busy schedule)?

    a. What changes can you make today that will stop letting those excuses keep you from being a seed sower?

Just an Ordinary Day

Just an ordinary day
Was how it all began,
But then I heard my Savior say
"I have a better plan!"

If you will listen to My voice
As daily tasks you face,
I'll show you opportunities
To share my love and grace.

For there are those who need to hear
I really love them so.
But I chose you to talk to them
That's what you need to know.

So please go on about your day
But keep your mind aware
That I may have a life for you
To touch and show you care.

It may be in your neighborhood,
At work or at the store,
Or it may be with those you love
Who need your patience more.

Oh yes, dear Lord, I want to be
A light for all to see
What God can do when in control
Of just one soul like me.

—Carol Hopson—
My Day His Way[3]

3

HIS HEART....

She Would be *Moved* with Compassion!

If you see some brother or sister in need and have the means to do something about it but turn a cold shoulder and do nothing, what happens to God's love? It disappears....
John 3 (THE MESSAGE)

As Christians, we all know it is our responsibility to love and share our faith with others. Yet loving people we don't really know (or worse, people we don't really like) can be quite a challenge. This is an area where most Christians could use some improvement. I believe that being moved to share Christ's love with others is a supernatural reaction that only God can deposit into your heart. On the subject of our heart, Ezekiel 36:26 says, "I will give you a new heart and put a new spirit in you; I will remove from you your heart of stone and give you a heart of flesh." Clearly, the Bible says there are two types of hearts in people; one of flesh and one of stone...interesting, huh? I once had someone pray over me for a "heart of flesh" and I wondered what that meant. Shortly after his prayer, my heart began a transformation of softening and feeling compassion for others in my community. I started to notice those hurting all around me and many times stepped out with an act of kindness as the Lord led me. I had never experienced anything like this before. I was one of those people who just didn't look closely at others because I was always in a hurry. I believe God gave me a new heart of compassion as a result of that simple prayer.

I believe there are many Christians who have developed a "heart of stone" and may not even realize it. They just aren't moved to do anything when they see a stranger in need. A heart of stone can develop after years of negative experiences, disappointments, or even abuse. Past painful experiences can be the one thing that starts the process of putting up walls that eventually hardens the heart. However, God can transform a hardened heart into a heart that responds to the needs of others.

A "heart of flesh" is what God desires to place into His people and is absolutely necessary for outreach to the world. A heart of flesh feels the pain of fellow man and acts in response. Jesus was the perfect example of a man who had a heart of flesh and was often moved with compassion for people. Jesus said in John 13:34 "a new command I give you: love one another. *As I have loved you*, so you must love one another." What did He mean "as I have loved you?" Let's take a closer look at Jesus' life and what it looked like when He was demonstrating His love for others.

MOVED WITH COMPASSION

When I recently started studying the book of Matthew, the Lord opened my eyes to an emotion that Jesus experienced time and time again. The words seemed to jump right off the pages of my Bible! I came across one passage after another of Jesus being *moved or filled with compassion.* The compassion that filled and moved Him resulted in extraordinary things happening on a daily basis. The Lord began to show me that compassion was a key component to Jesus' outreach ministry. Jesus let compassion move Him to fulfill the needs of others wherever He would go. Jesus didn't wait for the people to come to Him–He touched them where they were, even in the midst of a busy day.

Matthew 9:36 says, "when He [Jesus] saw the crowds, He had compassion on them, because they were harassed and helpless, like sheep without a shepherd." It's amazing that Jesus was fully man and fully God yet He felt the same emotions as you and I. The phrase moved with or felt compassion is found 12 times in the New Testament–9 out of 12 times it refers to Jesus. The definition of compassion is *a deep awareness of the suffering of another coupled with the wish to relieve* it.[4] Compassion is stronger than sympathy. It does more than just say, "I feel for you." Compassion captures the pain of another and moves our heart to do something about it. Many times, this results in *random acts of kindness.* In the New Testament, the term "He felt compassion" appears to be action-orientated that requires a willingness to engage brokenness, pain, suffering…even one's enemies or society's outcasts. We tend to save compassion for devastating events that are right in front of us such as 9/11, a hurricane, fires or tsunami. But we miss the smaller opportunities right in our own communities.

Jesus' was an example of one who lived His life full of compassion every day, and in every type of way. Let's look at some examples of what happened in Jesus' life when He was *moved or filled with compassion.*

In Matthew 9:36, we first read of Jesus experiencing compassion for the crowds. "When He saw the crowds, *He had compassion* on them, because they were harassed and helpless, like sheep without a shepherd." The interesting thing is that this verse tells us that Jesus did not view the people as just *a crowd*. He saw more than that. He saw each one of their individual needs and had compassion for them. In the next verse, He said to the disciples, "The harvest is plentiful but the workers are few. Ask the Lord of the harvest, therefore, to send out workers into His harvest field." Jesus refers to the harvest as "lives" and said to pray for more workers. Jesus saw the greatness of human need as not only an opportunity, but a harvest that was plentiful with not enough workers. The workers He refers to are followers of Christ. It wasn't for just the disciples, but a command for you and me. I wonder how many opportunities to meet human need get passed by daily because of the lack of willing laborers? Jesus saw this as a problem and actually instructed the disciples to pray for more help.

In Matthew 14:14, it says "When Jesus landed and saw a large crowd, *He had compassion* on them and healed their sick." In the verses to follow, we read a story about Him feeding 5,000+ people. They were hungry and Jesus made sure their physical needs were met that day. The interesting thing about this passage is that Jesus was actually trying to retreat to a solitary place to grieve the death of John the Baptist. Jesus had just heard the news that He was killed. He was simply trying to grieve the loss of a dear friend when the crowds found Him. Instead of being bothered by their presence, He had compassion on them. Jesus felt compassion, was moved by compassion, and let His compassion find its fulfillment in meeting the needs of others. Even though it wasn't the perfect time to reach out, He still put others ahead of His own needs and emotions and performed amazing miracles. How many times as women do we let our emotions dictate our lives and reactions to others?

Another example of what happened when Jesus experienced compassion is found in Mark 1:41. Jesus was "*moved with compassion*" and healed a leper! The way that Jesus healed this man was remarkable. To touch a leper in that day was unthinkable. Lepers were banished from society and people would not get even a stone's throw away from them. Lepers were the last people anyone would want to touch. Yet the first thing Christ did for this man was touch him. Jesus could have healed him first and then touched him. Recognizing his deepest need, Jesus stretched out His hand even before He spoke any words of healing. Sometimes acts of kindness to others will require taking a risk. That risk may not be as severe as catching a disease but rather, risking one's pride and/or fear of rejection. When you flow in Jesus' compassion for the world, you may risk reputation, pride, money, etc. How many times can you say that you were "moved with compassion" without weighing the risk involved? We tend to rationalize everything we do and in turn miss opportunities to be fully used by God. Jesus didn't do that. He was in tune with the Father's heartbeat and moved in compassion. Jesus prayed for more workers and He desires to use our hands to touch the lives of today's rejected people.

In Matthew 20:34, Jesus "*moved with compassion*" and healed two blind men along the side of the road. Jesus felt compassion and took costly action to touch lives. He did many things in His day that were unheard of or unacceptable. In Luke 7:11–15, Jesus touched the coffin of a widow's son and raised him from the dead. Remarkable things happened when our Lord was "moved with compassion" and this is His heart for us that we too would engage in Jesus' compassion ministry and touch lives in this generation.

LOVE IN ACTION

When Jesus was asked what the greatest commandment of all was, it included "love your neighbor as yourself." He was *commanding* us to love others. It was never an option or suggestion. Over the years, God has not told me that I must save so many people a month or else. What He has shown me over the years is to always look for opportunities to be used in His name. *We are His hands here on earth.* If we allow Him to direct our lives and move in the spirit, He will show us which lives we can affect and how. If we see a need and don't do anything to help, how will that further the kingdom or bring glory to God? My husband used to work in downtown Los Angeles and was once confronted with a situation that he could have ignored, or give a person in need a helping hand. Mike was crossing the street to go to lunch when he noticed a homeless man in a wheelchair stuck in the intersection. The light was about to turn green for the other cars to go! Mike ran over and helped him put the wheel back on the wheelchair that had fallen off and pushed him to safety. Many people ignored this man and kept right on walking. Mike did what Jesus would have done...he helped another person in need.

    When my daughter Alexis was little, I witnessed her young heart being moved with compassion. We were at the park one day riding bikes when we noticed a family that looked a little different. They had the appearance of being a family in need. Their clothes were old and worn out and they appeared to be living in a motor home parked in the parking lot. Their kids were running around playing at the park. One of the kids in particular, would stop and stare at my kids as they rode their bikes past them. I heard him say at one point, "I wish I had a bike." I told Alexis what the boy said and the first words out of her mouth were, "He can have my bike!" I didn't tell her what he said so that she would respond in such a generous way. I just wanted her to realize how lucky she was to have her own bike. When I asked her why she would want to give up her bike she said, "Because that's what Christians do." It was such a natural response. I was very proud of her. However, I have to admit that my flesh got in the way and I did not let her give the bike away.

It is God's desire that we touch lives with Him. He doesn't want anyone to live in eternity apart from Him and neither should we. We should make it our goal to take as many people to heaven with us as we can. However, many people in this generation are skeptical and on the defense when they sense you want to share Jesus with them. Take a step back in some of your relationships and try to see the person through the eyes of Jesus. What can you do to help them take a small step towards Him? If you truly believe that they would be better off knowing Jesus, introduce them to Him by being Christ-like, full of love and always available to help. This often happens in the context of a genuine relationship with that person. I recently heard that we each have 70 relational experiences a year. That is 70 potential opportunities to plant seeds in another person's life! (I believe that a busy woman actually has more than that.) I have found that taking the time to get to know the person and embracing them with an act of kindness is the best way to break down the walls of suspicion. When we do something unexpected for someone, they are caught off guard and are touched. We do this with no hidden agenda. I guarantee if you spend time in developing friendships with people that you normally wouldn't because they don't believe the same as you, one day you will have an opportunity to share Jesus with them. It is funny how these people can feel the urge to get back to church just from hanging around Christians (without us even saying anything). This is the power of the Holy Spirit at work through us.

JESUS' COMPASSION MINISTRY

When we engage in Jesus' compassion ministry walls start crumbling and opportunities to lead others to Christ present themselves. I believe compassion is going to be key to the end-time harvest. We have something to hope for and need to share it with the rest of the world. Time is running short and now is the time to be looking for opportunities to touch lives daily. God may use you daily, weekly or once in a while. The important thing is to be ready and alert for the opportunities and people He brings before you. Jesus had compassion for the crowds and was moved to relieve their suffering. Whether it be to forgive someone's sins, heal a leper or deliverance; Jesus responded to the hurting people around Him. Jesus didn't just feel sorry for the people. The compassion He felt compelled Him into love-empowered actions. Jesus even stopped midstride to heal a woman with a bleeding disorder. Jesus' compassion changed lives!

As we look at Jesus' ministry on earth, we see that He was out amongst the people. He lived life day-to-day as we do—out in the world. He didn't save His message of good news for special occasions or rent huge coliseums and wait for people to come to Him. He went to the people and demonstrated who He was. While His disciples just saw the crowds and wanted to turn them away, Jesus saw hurting and broken people in need of a Savior. As Christians, we have eternity to look forward to with Jesus. This is good news that we need to share with the rest of the world. Again, if we don't take the time to engage in the ministry of Jesus and reach out to the lost and hurting people of this world, then who will? Really...who? Jesus commands us to share the good news; to do less is letting our God down. We need to make a decision to stop living comfortable Christian lives and fully submit ourselves to furthering the kingdom while there is still time. Our time on this earth is very short and there are a lot of people who can be reached if we let God use us. As believers, we are the vessels that bring Jesus into the lives of unbelievers. The way our Lord chooses to bring himself glory is through His servants' hands.

Steps to engaging in Jesus' compassion ministry:

1 John 3:18 says, "...let us not love with words or tongue but with actions and in truth."

1. Stay close to the Father's heart. This is the most important way that you will be able to live a life that is walking in Jesus' compassion for the world. It cannot be done in your own strength. You cannot give out to the world any more than you are currently experiencing. Your relationship with Jesus and how much time you spend with Him is crucial. Pray daily for Jesus' heart of compassion in your life.
2. Slow down and be aware of opportunities around you. Change your plans if you have to. Be available to be used along the way.
3. Make room for new people in your life. Are there people whom you constantly run into? These may be potential friendships that God is bringing to you. Never get to a point where you have enough friends.
4. Really listen to people and put yourself in their shoes. What would help them the most? Is it a physical, financial or spiritual need that you can provide or offer prayer for?
5. Get involved in compassion ministries at your church that reach the community.

In this generation, it is not enough for us to merely be friendly or nice Christians. Instead, allow the Holy Spirit to pour out Jesus' compassion from our lives into the lives of others in our communities. Once you regain Jesus' compassion for the lost in your life, reaching out will become more natural. As you strive to become more like Jesus, meditate on Ephesians 5 from The Message Bible. It is an excellent example of how to live an extravagant life of love.

"Watch what God does, and then you do it, like children who learn proper behaviors from their parents. Mostly what God does is love you. Keep company with Him and learn a life of love. Observe how Christ loved us. His love was not cautious but extravagant. He didn't love in order to get something from us but to give everything of himself to us. Love like that."

OUR HEART'S RESPONSE

Read Mark 1:40-45

1. Have you ever been *moved with compassion* to help another person in need? What happened?

2. Jesus took great risks in reaching out to people society had banned. What are you afraid to risk by reaching out to others?

Read 2 Timothy 1:7

3. What does this verse say about fear? Who gives us a spirit of fear?

4. What steps can you take today to overcome your fears of outreach?

Compassion's Way

May I have your healing touch
And walk compassion's way
May each life that touches mine
Be filled with Yours today
—Jayne Houghton—

4

HIS HEART...

She Would Spend Time with Me

But when you pray, go into your room, close the door and pray to your Father, who is unseen. Then your Father, who sees what is done in secret, will reward you.
Matthew 6:6

In the previous chapter, we studied the life of Jesus and the many times He was *moved or filled with compassion.* This supernatural compassion resulted in Jesus doing remarkable things in the lives of many people. I believe that a heart of compassion (like Jesus had) is not only key, but crucial in becoming a busy woman who impacts others for Christ. Let's face it, if you really don't care about people in your community, you're not going to do anything about their needs. Sure you can force yourself to appear to care about people, but they will read right through you! I have found that when I take the time to *sit* with Jesus in my quiet times of prayer and meditation of His Word, my heart begins to change.

Not only do I start feeling compassion for people's needs around me, but I am often compelled to do something about it. In essence, my heart begins to mirror Jesus' heart for the world. I admit that I did not experience this type of compassion until I made a concerted effort to spend time with Jesus. After I made the commitment to spend time with Jesus, I began to see positive changes in my life. These changes not only benefited me personally, but also my family and often the lives of others in my community!

I believe that as Christian women, we can feel that we are too busy to stop and spend quiet time with Jesus. I know that I used to think that God would understand that I just didn't have time to meet with Him. Sure, I would offer up prayers during the day, but I never sat still long enough to hear His answers. God really does want to be your friend and support. We all know from experience that friendships don't flourish on one-sided conversations! I would use the excuses of work, mothering young children, volunteering and fatigue for not being available to sit with Jesus. I didn't realize at the time that I was too busy NOT to spend time with Him. I missed the very idea that I could regain the strength I needed to get through my most stressful of days by just sitting before Him. I should have listened to His leading all those years and sat with Him in a quiet place. Instead, I had it all turned around. I wasted a lot of years trying to do things on my own strength, when I could have leaned more on Him to carry my burdens. I can still remember those days when I was so overwhelmed with motherhood and would try to read my Bible at night right before I went to bed. I would get my pajamas on, wash my face, and crawl into bed with my Bible. Usually, within a few minutes of reading, my eyes would become so heavy that I would end up falling asleep. I would then wake up in the morning so disappointed at myself that I couldn't even stay awake to read the Bible! Then the guilt would set in. It was a cycle that I had a hard time breaking out of.

In this chapter, we will discuss the importance of spending quiet times with the Lord, the benefits of that time and the most common hindrances that keep busy women from being still before the Lord.

INTIMACY WITH JESUS = SPIRITUAL MATURITY

For years I literally felt God's still small voice calling me into a deeper intimacy with Him, but I gave Him every excuse on why I didn't have enough time to just sit with Him. God was trying to show me during those years that He could not fully reveal His plan and purpose for my life until I matured spiritually. The closer I got to the Lord, the more I wanted to find out what my purpose was on this earth and how He was going to use me to make a difference. The only way I could spiritually mature was through an intimate relationship with Jesus. This meant that I needed to study Jesus' nature and get to know Him personally and the only way to do that was by spending time with Him! God has a plan and a purpose for your life that He cannot release until you are spiritually mature. The reality is that unless we are maturing spiritually, we probably won't even seek the Lord on what His plans and purposes are for our lives. The only way to become equipped for outreach ministry is to recognize the voice of the Lord and where He is leading you. By going to church each week, we can grow in intellectual knowledge of the Bible, but unless we really get to know who Jesus is and unless we spend time seeking His presence, we will never fully know Him and mature spiritually.

The key to intimacy with Jesus Christ is spending time at His feet. This means spending quiet time in prayer and meditation of His Word. The Bible tells us in Matthew 6:6, *"When you pray, go into your room, close the door and pray to your Father, who is unseen. Then your Father who sees what is done in secret, will reward you."* God will reward you with peace and fulfillment. The act of really seeking God unlocks the mysteries of how He sees you and the world around you. God loves us! He longs for this kind of fellowship with His children. He is our *Abba Father*. The God of this universe desires time with His children and is not satisfied with short visits far and in between. He wants all of us, not just our leftovers. We need to set time aside for Him daily in order to allow Him to give us strength to make it through our busy days.

So many people are missing the real purpose of their life by not truly seeking out God's plan. Jeremiah 29:11–14 says, "'For I know the plans I have for you,' declares the LORD, 'plans to prosper you and not to harm you, plans to give you hope and a future. Then you will call upon me and come and pray to me, and I will listen to you. You will seek me and find me when you seek me with all your heart. I will be found by you,' declares the LORD." God promises over and over again in the Bible that when we seek Him–we will find Him! He is not a God who hides from us, He desires relationship with us.

God also calls us to be lights in this dark world. Matthew 5:13–16 says, "You are the salt of the earth. But if the salt loses its saltiness, how can it be made salty again? It is no longer good for anything, except to be thrown out and trampled by men. You are the light of the world. A city on a hill cannot be hidden. Neither do people light a lamp and put it under a bowl. Instead they put it on its stand, and it gives light to everyone in the house. In the same way, let your light shine before men, that they may see your good deeds and praise your Father in heaven." Our lives should shine with God's presence and draw people to us and it is then that we can share our faith.

God wants us to be hot for Him, and not passive. Revelation 3:15 says, "I know your deeds, that you are neither cold nor hot. I wish you were either one or the other! So, because you are lukewarm–neither hot nor cold–I am about to spit you out of my mouth." Just think about how many more believers there would be in this world if Christians would step out of their comfort zones and become active followers of Jesus and His purposes. We can't afford to settle for passive Christian lives if we want to make a difference in this world! Just the thought that the God of the universe loves His people so much should move us. He desires an intimate relationship with *you*! He wants to show us things that we may need to change in our lives. When we have a pure heart and are obedient to God's discipline, then He can fully use us. We are a work in progress.

READY, SET...SIT!

Having a Mary Heart in a Martha World, by Joanna Weaver, really jump started my quiet times with the Lord. I would highly recommend it if you are struggling with finding intimacy with Christ in the busyness of life. In the book, the author says that "Christianity is a process and not an event. It is a journey, not a destination."[6] Those words gave me some comfort. If our ultimate goal is to be like Jesus, we won't be able to escape the process it takes to become the type of Christian women God desires us to be.

You may be asking yourself–*why* is it so hard to commit to a daily time with the Lord? After all, He is our Lord and Savior. Why wouldn't we want to please Him by giving Him our time? Yet the reality is that your day is filled with things that can take precedence over quiet time. Or maybe you are like me and the more you don't set aside time with the Lord, the harder it is to get back into it. If you have a plan of action to jump start the habit of spending time at Jesus' feet you will have more success. It really does need to become a habit and part of your day. It needs to be a planned event just like anything else that takes your time.

The first thing you need to do is commit to a certain time of day that works best for you. If you are a morning person, getting up 30 minutes earlier each day could be a great option for you. The Bible gives us an example in Mark 1:35 of Jesus waking up early and finding a quiet place to pray by Himself. If you are a mom, a good time to spend with the Lord could be when your kids are in school or napping. When my children were young and took naps, I would spend the first 20–30 minutes of the nap in quiet time. I also had to make a conscious effort to not let the household chores distract me from putting this time first. When I made it a priority to do my quiet time first, somehow the rest of the housework got done. When I did the housework first, I ran out of time to spend with the Lord. Put some thought into a realistic time frame that you can commit to the Lord daily. Keep that time sacred and don't answer the phone or do housework. That can usually wait until you are done. Start your day with a prayer. Ask the Lord to show you what things need to get done and what can wait. Seek His guidance during the day when you feel overwhelmed with to-do stuff. If we put Him first, our days will be more productive. I have lived it and know that the days I have my quiet time, I'm more patient and nicer to be around.

The main focus of your quiet time is to worship the Lord, pray, read the Bible and *listen*. Remember, the Bible is spiritual food you can't live without if you want to grow in your relationship with Jesus. I have a special chair in my bedroom with a basket next to it for my quiet time. In the basket, I have a Bible, journal, pen and highlighter. I also have a few Bible study books that I am working on. I start my quiet time with listening to a couple worship songs and sometimes sing along as an act of worship. By putting worship first, it helps to clear my mind. God also says that He inhabits the praises of His people and most times I can sense His presence. Paul wrote in Philippians 4:6–7, "Do not be anxious about anything, but in everything, by prayer and petition, with thanksgiving, present your requests to God. And the peace of God which transcends all understanding, will guard your hearts and your minds in Christ Jesus." We should always thank Him for what He has done before we offer up our prayer requests. Also, during your quiet time, you are fixing your eyes on what is unseen. 2 Corinthians 4:16–18 says, "Therefore we do not lose heart. Though outwardly we are wasting away, yet inwardly we are being renewed day by day. For our light and momentary troubles are achieving for us an eternal glory that far outweighs them all. So we fix our eyes not on what is seen, but on what is unseen. For what is seen is temporary, but what is unseen is eternal." We refocus on what is really important when we look through supernatural eyes. We then have a new peace as we realize that no matter what comes our way, we can handle it because we have life in a healthy perspective.

A few more ideas you can try for designing your own quiet time is to read your Bible during breakfast and/or lunch. While I ate my lunch I replaced watching television with reading the Bible. Another great idea is to take a walk and talk to God while you exercise. I sometimes listen to sermons on my iPod when I walk. Going to the park or coffee shop for an hour a few times a week to read your Bible is another idea. Also, buy a small Bible that fits into your purse and read it whenever you have a few minutes while you are out and about. Whatever you choose to do, just be consistent. I promise that God will meet you and your spiritual hunger will begin to grow. Once you start the habit of spending time with the Lord, you will look forward to it. Remember, don't feel guilty if you skip a day. God will still be waiting for you the next day. Take small realistic chunks of time at first and build from there. Start with at least 20 minutes a day if you can. Keep in mind, habits take time to form. Spending time with the Lord is a good habit that you want to develop, but it does take some discipline.

THE BENEFITS OF SPENDING TIME WITH JESUS

When you spend regular quiet time with Jesus, positive changes are going to begin to happen in your life. For instance, you are going to develop a spiritual hunger for the Word that you may have never had before. The Bible becomes like spiritual food to your soul. It is a different kind of appetite than with regular food. With regular food, you feel hungry, eat and then are satisfied. With spiritual food, the more you read God's Word, the bigger your appetite will become. I'm an example of this happening in my own life. When I made the commitment to read the Bible each day, it became so much more relevant and alive to me the more I read it. Going to church on Sunday without any time during the week in quiet time at the feet of Jesus is going to keep you in baby-Christian mode. You won't fully grow into a mature Christian woman of God until you take steps to feed yourself. A 30-minute sermon each week is not enough spiritual food so that we grow at the rate God wants us to. If we rely solely on Sunday morning service for our spiritual food, it will take more than a lifetime for us to fully mature into powerful women God can use to impact a generation! You need Sunday mornings at church for fellowship and the Word, but you need more than that to develop into a fully mature woman of God.

Another huge benefit is that you will learn to recognize God's voice. During your quiet time God can speak to you in different ways–a still small voice, a thought, an impression or a Bible verse. Without a quiet time, that thought, voice or impression will be drowned out by the busyness of the day. When the Lord speaks to me, it comes as a flood of thoughts while I am praying and worshiping Him. I have a journal and

Purposes Of His Heart

I write down thoughts that I later read as encouraging words from the Lord. He also speaks through the Bible. Sometimes I will have a certain verse pop into my head and when I look it up, it is exactly the encouragement I needed. Occasionally, I just open the Bible and start reading and can come across a verse that hits me like an arrow. I also use devotional books that provide more structure to my Bible reading time. Additionally, most Bibles have a reading plan to help you read throughout the year. Dedicating time out of your busy schedule to spend with the Lord is going to result in amazing changes in your life.

The first change you will notice as a direct result of spending time with the Lord is a clearer understanding of who God is. Remember God's Word is His love letter to us. If you want to know God's thoughts, to hear His heart, to have His presence be a part of your everyday life, then read God's Word. Everything that God wants to say to you is recorded in the Bible…straight from His heart to yours. 2 Timothy 3:16 says, "All scripture is God-breathed and is useful for teaching, rebuking, correcting and training in righteousness, so that the man of God may be thoroughly equipped for every good work." As we draw closer to God, His heart will be revealed to us. As you seek His face, He will change your heart to be like His. As a result, you will have more compassion and love for others. You will also experience more joy in life by really knowing the living God and understanding your purposes here on earth. Kent Hughes puts it this way. "Our lives are like photographic plates, and prayer is like a time exposure to God. As we expose ourselves to God for a half hour, an hour, perhaps two hours a day, His image is imprinted more and more upon us. More and more we absorb the image of His character, His love, His wisdom, His way of dealing with life and people."[5]

Another change in your life that you can expect as a result of intimate fellowship with Christ is the release of

His power and confidence in your life. In Acts 3, there is a great story of Peter and John reaching out in an act of kindness to a crippled man at the temple gate. He was asking for money when the men offered Him something worth far more than that. These men had enough confidence to tell a man who had been crippled since birth to get up and walk in Jesus' name...and he did! Acts 4:13 is a picture of how others viewed these apostles. It says that "when they saw the courage of Peter and John and realized that they were unschooled, ordinary men, they were astonished and they took note that these men had been with Jesus." Did you notice that they were just "unschooled, ordinary men?" They were ordinary men who became rock stars of their community! It is a natural response that other people will be able to see Jesus in you the more time you spend with Him. As you experience more confidence in Christ's power available to you, it will increase your desire to reach out in more situations. You will have a new boldness to live your life as an example and lead others to Christ.

According to 1 Corinthians 12, we all have a place in the body of Christ in which to use our gifts and talents. By spending time with God, He can reveal to you what your talents and purposes are. It is a reality that a handful of preachers are not going to reach the whole world but through people like you and me who are willing to do one-to-one ministry in our communities. If during your quiet time you focus on overcoming the internal obstacles to doing God's work, you will never lack for ministry to others. God's fullness in you will naturally flow into the lives of others.

HINDRANCES TO HAVING A QUIET TIME

From experience, I know that there are going to be daily hindrances that will keep you from spending time with Jesus. I have struggled with this for years and speak from experience. I assure you, if you can acknowledge and work through these hindrances, you will reap the benefits of a regular meeting with the Lord. I promise that spending time with the Lord will be something that you won't want to go a day without! Put your eyes on Jesus every day as He is our perfect example of living a life that pleased the Father. He was never in a hurry. He knew who He was and where He was going. He wasn't held hostage to the world's (or the home's!) demands.

One of the hindrances is that we put work before worship. For some reason I have always felt that I had to have *everything* done on my daily to-do list before I could have my quiet time. Each morning would start with good intentions to have a quiet time when the kids napped or were in school. Once they were asleep or gone, I noticed every single thing that needed to be done in my house first. I would empty the dishwasher, load the dishwasher, do a load of laundry, make a phone call, check my e-mail, and oh yeah, wipe down the kitchen counter! Then I was ready, but by then, the kids were awake! I had to learn to look past the housework and make time with the Lord a priority. We each have our own distractions, mine was the housework. I had to learn that the housework could wait. Your distractions can include any of the following: television, cell phone, Internet, or E-mail. Whatever it is, acknowledge it and reprioritize. I think Satan knows our weak spots and there was a reason why I was most bothered with the condition of my house right before my time with the Lord. Of course, Satan wants to interfere and keep us from experiencing real growth and will use whatever distraction is necessary.

In fact, he often uses work as a distraction. When we put work before worship, we put the cart before the horse. The cart is important; so is the horse. But the horse must come first, or we end up pulling the cart ourselves. Frustrated and weary, we can nearly break under the pressures of service, for there is always something that needs to be done. When we first spend time in His presence–when we take time to hear His voice– God provides the horsepower we need to pull the heaviest load.[6]

Another hindrance is accepting the lie that you aren't worthy of spending time at Jesus' feet. It may have been several years since you made it a priority to spend time with Jesus in an intimate way, so you may feel like it is too late. Maybe you feel like you have blown it too many times with the way you have handled life and feel guilty. It is true that the closer we get to Jesus, the more we realize we have a long way to go to becoming more Christ-like. Our sin is exposed when we get close to Him. The good news is that He is faithful and just to forgive us when we mess up and we can move on. Psalm 32:2,5 says, "Blessed is the man whose sin the Lord does not count against him....Then I acknowledged my sin to you and did not cover up my iniquity. I said, 'I will confess my transgressions to the Lord'–and you forgave the guilt of my sin." Any guilt that you are experiencing is NOT from the Lord! When you sin, ask for forgiveness, pray for strength to not sin again and *move on*! Don't get stuck in wallowing in your sin, because that is exactly where Satan wants you to camp out. Self condemnation has the potential of paralyzing a Christian from experiencing intimacy with Christ. I speak from experience. If you struggle with this, pray that the Lord will break that off of you. Don't let another day go by living in guilt over past sins.

In the past, there were times I felt that I messed up too much for God to use me. I especially felt this way during the demanding days of mothering my young children. I constantly compared myself to other mothers and never measured up in my own eyes. I realized that I wasn't a very patient mother to my children and struggled with much guilt on those days that I lost it. I needed my quiet time the most during those days to draw strength from the Lord. During those times He reminded me that He knew everything about me because He created me. Psalm 139 says "O LORD, you have searched me and you know me. You know when I sit and when I rise; you perceive my thoughts from afar. You discern my going out and my lying down; you are familiar with all my ways. Before a word is on my tongue you know it completely, O Lord." These verses assured me that God knew I was going to mess up before I did, but He still loves me. We are all a work in progress, with a lot of work to be done! Hebrews 4:16 says "Let us then approach the throne of grace with confidence, so that we may receive mercy and find grace to help us in our time of need." For our whole life we should strive to keep our relationship strong with the Lord.

The more time I spend with the Lord, the better person I want to be. I get convicted about some areas that I may slip up in that, otherwise, I wouldn't think anything about it. God convicts me every time I even slightly begin to gossip. I can't get away with anything! But I am maturing and learning to live like He wants me to along the way. No matter what you have done in the past, Jesus is waiting for you to return to an intimate relationship with Him. Being a Christian is not about religion, but relationship with Him. Don't get caught up in the rules and regulations of religion, but pursue intimacy with your Lord and Savior Jesus Christ.

The last hindrance we will talk about is that some of us have actually had a hunger for the Lord's presence and Word, but have lost that hunger. I know that was true for me in several seasons of my life. Joanna Weaver shares a perfect analogy of filling our hunger with other things as she shares a story about her friend's experience. "She tells of the story of having company over for dinner one night, She'd worked hard all day on a beautiful meal–four courses and a fancy dessert. It was going to be wonderful. Somewhere around the middle of the afternoon, Teri realized she was hungry.

"I'd been so busy with cooking and cleaning," she says, "I had completely missed lunch." It was only four o'clock and the guests weren't due until six. "I always keep a hidden stash of Snickers bars," she says with a grin. So she grabbed a couple of candy bars and sat down to rest, enjoying her clean living room and beautifully set table. "It did the trick! My stomach wasn't growling anymore. I was able to take my shower, do my hair, and get dressed with plenty of time to spare." It wasn't until Teri sat down to dinner that she discovered the problem. "There I was with that wonderful dinner I'd worked on all day to prepare, but my appetite was gone!" The midafternoon snack had taken the edge off her hunger. She ended up picking at her plate as she watched everyone else dig in, enjoying their meal. "The Lord spoke to me at that moment," Terry says. "He showed me that we often fill our lives with spiritual Snickers bars–things like friends, books, and shopping. They may be good things, completely innocent things–but not when they take the edge off our hunger for God."[6]

Does this resonate with you? I can think of a few things in my life that can easily take first place over intimacy with God. I am sure you can too. God is the only one who can permanently fill our empty souls with peace and contentment. Material things just don't fill us with lasting results. If you want real fruit in your life, then start making changes today. Put "spend time with God" at the top of your to-do list and watch your life and your family change for the better.

Meditate on God's promise in Isaiah 40:31 when you feel too overwhelmed to spend time with Him–"but those who hope in the Lord will renew their strength. They will soar on wings like eagles; they will run and not grow weary, they will walk and not be faint." Believe that the Lord wants to fellowship with you. He wants to make a home in each area of your heart. Robert Boyd Munger writes in *My Heart Christ's Home*, "Without question one of the most remarkable Christian doctrines is that Jesus Christ Himself through the presence of the Holy Spirit will actually enter a heart, settle down and be at home there."[7] I will end this chapter with a great analogy that Munger writes about when he invited Jesus into every area of his own heart. He describes each area of his heart as a "room" and accepts the invitation from Jesus to meet with Him in the living room.

The Living Room

> We walked next into the living room. This room was rather intimate and comfortable. I liked it. It had a fireplace, overstuffed chairs, a sofa, and a quiet atmosphere.
>
> He also seemed pleased with it. He said, "This is indeed a delightful room. Let us come here often. It is secluded and quiet, and we can fellowship together."
>
> Well, naturally as a young Christian I was thrilled. I couldn't think of anything I would rather do than have a few minutes with Christ in intimate companionship.
>
> He promised, "I will be here early every morning. Meet me here, and we will start the day together." So morning after morning, I would come downstairs to the living room and He would take a book of the Bible from the bookcase. He would open it and then we would read together. He would tell me of its riches and unfold to me its truths. He would make my heart warm as He revealed His love and His grace He had toward me. These were wonderful hours together. In fact, we called the living room the "withdrawing

room." It was a period when we had our quiet time together.

But, little by little, under the pressure of many responsibilities, this time began to be shortened. Why, I don't know, but I thought I was just too busy to spend time with Christ. This was not intentional, you understand; it just happened that way. Finally, not only was the time shortened, but I began to miss a day now and then. It was examination time at the university. Then it was some other urgent emergency. I would miss it two days in a row and often more.

I remember one morning when I was in a hurry, rushing downstairs, eager to be on my way.

As I passed the living room, the door was open. Looking in, I saw a fire in the fireplace and Jesus was sitting there. Suddenly in dismay I thought to myself, "He was my guest. I invited Him into my heart! He has come as Lord of my home. And yet here I am neglecting Him."

I turned and went in. With downcast glance, I said, "Blessed Master, forgive me. Have you been here all these mornings?"

"Yes," He said, "I told you I would be here every morning to meet with you." Then I was even more ashamed. He had been faithful in spite of my faithfulness. I asked His forgiveness and He readily forgave me as He does when we are truly repentant.

"The trouble with you is this: you have been thinking of the quiet time, of the Bible study and prayer time, as a factor in your own spiritual progress, but you have forgotten that *this hour means something to me also.*"⁷

OUR HEART'S RESPONSE

Read Luke 10:38–42

1. How does Jesus respond to Martha as she complains about her sister Mary?

2. Which sister do you most relate to? Why?

3. Where would be the perfect spot to spend time at Jesus' feet each day? What time would work best for your schedule?

4. What satisfies your spiritual hunger besides the Word of God (TV, relationships, shopping, hobbies, etc.)?

5. What are specific hindrances that you will have to overcome to prioritize time with the Lord each day?

    a. Pray that you can overcome these hindrances and consistently spend time with Jesus.

5

HIS HEART...

She Would Bless Others with Her God-given Gifts and Talents

Each one should use whatever gift He has received to serve others, faithfully administering God's grace in its various forms.
1 Peter 4:10

One of the most common struggles busy people face in the area of outreach is the belief that you have to posses certain spiritual gifts (such as the *gift of evangelism*) or be an educated Bible scholar to share Christ with others. Most people just don't feel equipped enough to share their faith. We have the fear that people will ask us questions we can't answer when we bring up the subject of Jesus. While these reasons for not sharing your faith sound valid, they are really just more excuses. For example, 1 Corinthians 1:27 says, "But God chose the foolish things of the world to shame the wise; God chose the weak things of the world to shame the strong." God chooses to use plain ordinary people in the world to touch one life at a time for Him. The truth is that there are many spiritual gifts and natural talents that God gave ordinary Christians which can be used to impact lives in this generation! You currently possess some of those abilities! We have a God who loves to give spiritual gifts to His own. He even put a plan together for your life before you were born and gave you the natural talents you would need to fulfill those purposes when He created you. In this chapter I will help you identify some of your own God-given gifts and talents. I will also share my story of when God activated my gifts and talents and how I use them today for the Lord's purposes. I encourage you to recognize that God had a plan when He created you that included impacting others with your gifts and talents. He gave you everything you need to fulfill His plan for your life. You are God's masterpiece! There is not one person on earth who is exactly like you.

A CHILD'S HEART

In previous chapters, I shared that supernatural compassion is absolutely necessary in reaching out to others. Compassion makes all the difference as to whether or not you will be compelled to do something about another person in need. Giving you a compassionate heart to be used along with your gifts and talents was part of God's original plan when He designed you. And that compassionate heart was evident early in your childhood. Take a few moments with me and reflect back to your childhood days on the school playground. As a child do you remember when someone on the school playground got hurt? Maybe they fell on the blacktop while running and skinned their knee. How many children ran to their side and were moved with compassion at the sight of their boo-boo? Do you remember that feeling you had when you saw another kid hurt? The hurt child didn't even have to be your friend—you just knew you had to help! Now picture the following scenario…which kid were you?

A group of kids are playing tag and one falls and skins his knee. The boy is crying really hard and compassion is instantly activated in all the children who just who saw it happen. The girl who has the gift of administration quickly goes into action and tells another kid who is good at follow through to run and get a teacher. The girl who would one day become a nurse grabs a napkin out of her lunch box and tries to stop the bleeding. The child gifted with being an encourager stays close to his side and offers words of comfort to the boy. Of course, the future pastors start praying! This is an example of kids moving in compassion for another person in need while operating in their early gifts (what came natural to them).

Kids have a natural way of responding to people in need. They don't consider the costs of reaching out and helping out one another, they let their heart lead them to do what is right. What has happened to all the grown-ups who were so eager to help someone who was hurt? It is harder to notice an adult who is hurting, but when you overheard conversations that indicated a need, did you respond or pretend you didn't hear? Compassion was originally part of your DNA! The unfortunate reality is that negative experiences of how others responded to our compassion (either verbal or nonverbal) as we grew up may have hardened our hearts and caused us to lose confidence. We are no longer compelled to do something about the needs of others without weighing the costs. But as I shared in previous chapters, that lost compassion can be regained by spending time with Jesus, who is the perfect example of one who let compassion fill His heart and move Him to help another in need.

EQUIPPED FOR PURPOSE

God has equipped us with all we need to impact the world with His love and compassion in a non-threatening way. I love the way The Message Bible translates Jesus' words in Matthew 10, "Jesus sent His twelve harvest hands out with this charge: 'Don't begin by traveling to some far off place to convert unbelievers. And don't try to be dramatic by tackling some public enemy. Go to the lost, confused people right here in the neighborhood. Tell them that the kingdom is here. Bring health to the sick. Raise the dead. Touch the untouchables. Kick out the demons. You have been treated generously, so live generously. Don't think you have to put on a fund-raising campaign before you start. You don't need a lot of equipment. *You are the equipment*, and all you need to keep that going is three meals a day. Travel light.'"

So what do you think Jesus meant when He said "you are the equipment?" One definition for *equipment* is *anything kept, furnished, or provided for a specific purpose.*[8] If God says we "are the equipment," that means He provides us with everything we need to fulfill His purposes. Matthew 10 is pretty specific on some of those purposes which include reaching out to the hurting, giving freely, praying for the sick, sharing the good news, casting out demons and even raising the dead! Most of us probably don't feel equipped enough to do all this, but Jesus said we have everything we need. In John 14:12–14 Jesus says "I tell you the truth, anyone who has faith in me will do what I have been doing. He will do *even greater things* than these, because I am going to the Father. And I will do whatever you ask in my name, so that the Son may bring glory to the Father. You may ask me for anything in my name, and I will do it." Jesus wants to use our lives in ways grander than we could ever imagine or settle for! He looks for *available* busy people to impact others in remarkable ways with Him. Just think, if we actually believed that and started going after more supernatural encounters with people in everyday life...that would be so exciting, not to mention how many people would be impacted for Christ!

I believe that God did indeed equip you at birth with everything you need to impact people for Him during your lifetime. God specially designed you the way He did because He needed someone just like you in this world right now to help fulfill some of His purposes in the lives of others. God chose this generation for you to impact.

DISCOVERING YOUR GIFTS AND TALENTS

Psalm 139:15–16 says, "My frame was not hidden from you when I was made in the secret place. When I was woven together in the depths of the earth, your eyes saw my unformed body. All the days ordained for me were written in your book before one of them came to be." According to these verses God designed you with much thought. No matter what the circumstances are on how you got here, you are no accident. The talents that you have were given to you because God had a plan for your life and it was for much more than you may have realized. Hobbies are great, but doing God's work is even better! Let's discover what some of those gifts and talents are in your life.

I believe there is a direct connection between what you were interested in as a child and what your gifts and talents are today. Your childhood is a great place to start in discovering your natural talents. Let's take a walk together down memory lane. I would like you to think for a few minutes about what you liked to play as a child. Did you like to play school? Many of my friends who did, became teachers. Did you like to read books? My uncle did and became an attorney. Did you spend hours playing and taking care of your dolls? I bet you turned out to be a great mom! Did you like to play with your friends' hair or do makeovers? My aunt did and she became a hairdresser. When you played store with your friend, were you the cashier or the shopper? No, shopping isn't a gift! If you were the cashier, maybe you have a career in retail or computers. Did you like to draw or write stories? My mom did and she has authored several books. Guess what I used to like to play? I loved to organize club meetings with the neighborhood kids. I would announce that we were having a club meeting and that all those who attended would get some free candy. I admit to bribery! Do you see a connection in your own childhood play and your profession or hobbies? Children are not afraid to do what comes natural to them and your childhood is a great place to examine some of your early gifts.

Have you ever heard someone say "she is such a good listener" or "she is so giving?" These are both gifts. Not everyone is good at listening (without interrupting) and not everyone is generous. There are so many gifts that can be used to bless others. What about people who have the gift of hospitality and can make you feel so welcomed in their home? My aunt has this gift and is always making us cookies when we come for a visit. Also, people with this gift throw the best parties! This is a very unique gift given from the Lord. If the idea of entertaining others makes you stressed out, that's okay. It may not be your gift, but the gift of hospitality isn't any more important than your gifts. God created you the way He did for a reason. His plans for your life may not include being the hostess of the year!

God made all of us, yet we are all so very different. Some people have used their gifts and talents in amazing ways. They have used their gifts and talents to start businesses, have great hobbies or create history-making inventions. Some people have even gone to school to learn how to further develop their gifts and talents. Do you ever find yourself measuring your gifts and talents and their importance against others in your life? We all do. The reality is that all gifts are equal in God's eyes. The world's standard has decided which ones deserve the most attention. I don't know about you, but I have found that when I'm helping others with my own gifts and talents, I find the most joy in life. It is a great feeling when you are helping someone else with what comes naturally to you. When you are operating in your gifts, it's often easy and fulfilling.

Outreach to others doesn't have to be a hard task when you are operating the way God created you to be. God gave us gifts and talents in order to fulfill His purpose for our lives. As each person's purpose in life is fulfilled in a different way, we need different gifts to do that. Maybe God's purpose for you is to bless others with music, so He gave you a beautiful voice or a talent to play an instrument well. God may have given you the gift of teaching so you can become a teacher at school or church. Not everyone can sing, nor teach. These are true gifts. Don't underestimate your gifts and the important role they play in reaching out to touch the lives of others.

Some people are actually blessed enough to be in professions where God uses their gifts and talents to earn a living. These are the people who just love their jobs. They are doing what God created them to do. The bonus is that as they become more and more successful in their careers, they can give more money to their church or to ministries that are furthering the kingdom. Also, business men and women have a large group of people to reach out to that the church may never reach.

There is a lie that Satan has been circulating for years and has been construed as truth in the minds of many. That lie says that unless your ministry is done within the walls of the church, it's not considered ministry. For example, I have a friend who is a school teacher and she always had the desire to one day become a missionary and finally "do ministry." One day God opened her eyes to the reality that her ministry was right before her in the lives of the children she taught each day. All along, she operated in her gifts and talents in the ministry field God had planned for her. She just didn't realize it. It was an eye-opening experience and she became more intentional to impact the kids in her mission field which was her classroom. Once she realized she was "doing ministry," she found more joy and contentment in her job.

Where you are in life right now is not a mistake but rather, part of God's specific plan for your life. God has placed accountants, salespeople, teachers, moms, volunteers, etc. all in strategic places in the world to make a difference where they are planted. If evangelism only happened at outreach events or Sunday mornings, "saving the world" would be a job too big for the church. There is not enough advertising that a church could do in order to reach the same amount of people the body of Christ comes into personal contact with each and every day! God's plan for saving souls in the world is to use people like you in everyday life sharing His love with others–one life at a time. The unique gifts and talents you have been born with were given to you so that you could impact people every day–whether at home, work, school or in the community. The key is an awareness that you truly are gifted enough to impact lives for the kingdom. Remember that your gifts may not look the same as the person giving a testimony on Sunday morning. There was a young man at my church who shared how he was bold in sharing Christ with young people out in the marketplace. I thought, there is no way I could be that bold. I began to even downplay what I was doing in my community. God reminded me that He was using this young man to reach people I could never reach and vice versa. Do you really think a busy mom would stop and talk with him on the streets if he was street witnessing? Probably not...but she would most likely accept an invitation to my Bible study if I took time to get to know her first. Do you see my point? God uses different people in different ways but all with the same purpose…to draw others to Him. You cannot compare gifts, because each person is uniquely gifted for the place in life that God has ordained for them individually. The Message Bible says in 1 Corinthians 12, "God's various gifts are handed out everywhere; but they all originate in God's Spirit. God's various ministries are carried out everywhere; but they all originate in God's Spirit…. Each person is given something to do that shows who God is: Everyone gets in on it, everyone benefits. All kinds of things are handed out by the Spirit to all kinds of people!... All these gifts have a common origin, but are handed out one by one by the one Spirit of God. He decides who gets what, and when."

YOUR OWN STYLE

Just as God made each of us uniquely, we are all going to operate in outreach differently (or at least we should). I believe this is actually good news for Christians who have thought they could never do outreach. We have all been stuck in the belief that outreach must look a certain way or it's not ministry. This is really putting God in a box and we should not put limitations on the way He chooses to use us.

For example, the way I reach out to my community may look completely different than the way you reach yours. Each community may have different needs. The important thing is that we all have the same purpose in mind which is to share Christ's love and compassion and message of hope to the world. The way I have used my gifts and talents for God's purposes is through Bible study groups I have started for moms at my children's public school. I'm using my administrative gift. My purpose of starting these groups is to invite other women who may not attend church to come join us for fellowship and studies. I see my group as a stepping stone to draw women into a personal relationship with Jesus and encourage them to take their family to church. (Remember I liked organizing club meetings as a child!) I didn't realize I was also an evangelist until I started these groups. My heart grew with a desire to share Christ with more people as I saw lives transformed. I also volunteered as outreach director at my church for several years and planned outreach events to give church members opportunities to share the Lord with the community. While these are only some of the most recent ways I have used my gifts and talents, I know that there are more that I have yet to open and use. The Bible says that as we are good stewards with what God has given us, more we will be given. One gift being activated often leads to the activation of another. I recently realized this to be true in my own life as I spent time thinking about the experiences I have had in unlocking some of my gifts and talents.

One day I spent some time before the Lord reflecting back on times in my life when I felt that certain gifts or talents were activated. I even went as far back as my childhood and was surprised to get a great God perspective on when each gift was first opened. As I spent time that day reflecting on my experiences, the Lord gave me the following analogy of my life as seen through the eyes of God:

Tiffany was born in Southern California in a generation I knew would listen to her as she shared My heart. She was born with a somewhat shy disposition and a very quiet voice. As she grew up, she learned to speak louder so people could hear her. This helped her to overcome her shy nature. When she was a little girl and was old enough to make friends on her own, I moved her family to Bakersfield, California. I moved her family to a part of town that was under new construction. Shortly after moving there I activated her gifts of boldness and deep desire to make new friends. The unlocking of these gifts prompted Tiffany to embark on a crusade of knocking on the door of every house on the street and asking, "Do you have any kids I can play with?"

After a few years of getting comfortable with her new neighborhood friends, I unlocked Tiffany's gift of administration and planted an idea to start a club. The neighborhood kids responded favorably to Tiffany's gift of leadership and came to the first club meeting. Tiffany was so excited to be leading a group that she let the time get away from her. The saying, "Time flies when you're having fun" was true for Tiffany that day! Her enthusiasm resulted in kids deciding they didn't want to come back because the meeting lasted too long! But Tiffany got a taste of her early gifting as a leader and liked it! She also learned a valuable lesson to be respectful of others' time and schedule.

Another gift Tiffany would tap into early in her childhood was when she was given a tape recorder. She would record her own voice for hours pretending to broadcast a live newscast. She didn't know it, but she was practicing her gift of speaking.

Tiffany was raised in a Christian home and was always eager to invite her friends to go to church with her. She would look forward to altar calls when she could ask her friends if they wanted to go forward to accept Jesus as their personal Savior. This was her early childhood experience of operating in her evangelistic gift.

Tiffany's friendly personality brought her many friends during her childhood, but she had difficulty finding any who were loyal. She felt left out of friendships at school on many occasions. This was a part of My plan to develop Tiffany's sensitivity to other people's feelings. The gift of compassion for others was also beginning to form in her heart.

I arranged for Tiffany to meet her husband at a very young age; she was 15 and he was 17 when they first met. She never imagined that Mike was one she would marry and she actually thought he was a "nerd" at the time! I had the last laugh when they married in 1990. I blessed Tiffany and Mike with three beautiful children.

I placed the Milbys in Placentia with the divine purpose for them to impact lives in their community for Me. Upon relocating, I gave Tiffany the idea that she should run for president of the Placentia MOMS Club®. This was part of the plan that she would start a Bible study for moms just a few years later. This group was a tool I used to bring Kim to me just three weeks before her death. The death of Tiffany's friend changed her life forever. Her gift of having a heart for the lost was ignited and the boldness she once had as a little girl returned. She began to invite every mom she knew to the group. Her gift of teaching was opened during this time as she taught the women life lessons from the Bible.

Tiffany's gift of evangelism grew tremendously during this season and compelled her to start an outreach ministry at her church. The gift of evangelism that had been dormant for several years was used to touch thousands of lives with the gospel in a short period of time.

In 2006, I began to open the gift of writing in Tiffany and the idea to write this book was birthed within her."

Have you ever wondered what your story is from God's point of view? When you are done reading this chapter, please take some time to review the questionnaire in Appendix B so that you too can recognize the gifts God has activated in your life. I believe that God will also show you your story through His eyes.

USE WHAT YOU'VE GOT!

The Bible says in the parable found in Matthew 25 that the more talents we use, the more we will be given. Talents in this passage can represent any resource that God has given us. Matthew 25:21 says, "His master [God] replied, 'Well done, good and faithful servant [us]! You have been faithful with a few things; I will put you in charge of many things. Come and share your master's happiness!'" This verse tells me that God is very happy when we use what He has given us and often rewards us with more responsibility. On the other hand, Matthew 25:26 is a picture of God angry and upset that we didn't use what He gave us. You see, the more we use, the more He will give us. Using one gift often opens up another.

What are you doing with the gifts God so generously gave you? Are you using them to make Him look good? A listening ear, a caring heart, a handyman, a good cook…are all gifts that can touch unbelievers' hearts so they take notice of Jesus demonstrated through your life. Jesus said He would "draw all men unto Him" and if people see Jesus in you, they can't help but take notice. They will ask you questions. Please stop comparing your gifts and talents with others! It really is a waste of time. Everyone was made differently and one gift is not better than the other in God's eyes. It's what you do with it that makes Him smile. The purpose of your gifts is to use them to make God look good. When you use your gifts to serve others, you will feel the most fulfilled. God made you that way.

When you reach out and operate in your natural gifts, the amount of fear to share Christ's love and compassion with others should be minimal. Once you identify your gifts and do what God made you for, the more comfortable you become. God may use several people to plant seeds in someone's life before he or she accepts Christ as Savior. I love what The Message Bible says in Ephesians 2, "Saving is all His idea, and all His work. All we do is trust Him enough to let Him do it. It's God's gift from start to finish! We don't play the major role. If we did, we'd probably go around bragging that we'd done the whole thing! No, we neither make nor save ourselves. God does both the making and saving. He *creates each of us by Christ Jesus to join Him in the work He does,* the good work He has gotten ready for us to do, work we had better be doing." You're a partner with the Lord in the work He has already started in someone's life.

Review the list of gifts and talents in Appendix A and specific ways that you can use them to share Christ's love and compassion and message of hope with others. This is a great way to identify your gifts. The list will help you think about creative ways to use your gifts and talents for others. You may even have gifts that are so unique they aren't even listed. Think about what you are good at and how you can use that to glorify God today.

In your quiet time ask God to show you the gifts or talents He has given you. Once you have identified your gifts and talents and realize that you have a purpose to use them to touch lives for Christ, you are a powerful force that threatens Satan's plans to take as many people to hell with him as he can! You may have gifts and talents that have laid dormant for years. If you were discouraged to use your gifts and talents as a kid, you may have buried them. Also, due to negative experiences of comparing your gifts and talents you may have dismissed what God has given you. It is now time to re-examine what God has given you even as a child. Go back down memory lane and try to remember what you used to love as a child and what came natural to you. What are you doing when you feel most fulfilled? These are great indications of what your gifts and talents are. Don't let Satan discourage you another day! You are a uniquely gifted child of God capable of impacting a generation for Christ!

OUR HEART'S RESPONSE

Read Romans 12:6–8

1) What are the specific areas of gifts that are mentioned in these passages?

2) Do you identify yourself as possessing any of these gifts? Remember each gift can operate in a number of ways. (For example, if you have the gift of serving, you can serve others at church, school, family or community in various ways.)

3) To help you further identify your gifts and talents, think about the following:

    a) What was your favorite thing to play as a child?
    b) What or who are you most passionate about?
    c) What are you doing when you feel the most fulfilled?
    d) What would your friends say your gifts and talents are? What are you good at?

4) In what specific ways do you think you can use your gifts and talents to share Christ's love and compassion with others? (Be creative.)

5) Read Matthew 25:31–46. How does God feel when we overlook or ignore people in need? How do these verses make you feel?

6

HIS HEART...

She Would Produce "Good Fruit" in Her Life

*She will be like a tree planted by the water that
sends out its roots by the stream. It does not fear
when heat comes; its leaves are always green. It has
no worries in a year of drought
and never fails to bear fruit.*
Jeremiah 17:8

Is it possible to become a busy woman who is good at the balancing act of living life with a full schedule while incorporating outreach to others? Can we really become busy *yet* balanced Christian women? Of course we can! Even though Satan will try everything he can to discourage you to the point of physical and mental exhaustion to render you as a non-threat, you still have the power through the Holy Spirit to take control over your own life. You are the only one who has control over your thoughts, reactions and physical body, regardless of how others push your buttons! You can learn to recognize the enemy's schemes that can steer you down the path of physical and mental exhaustion that leaves you ineffective in reaching out to others. Today is the perfect day to put a stake in the ground and proclaim that your busyness will not produce any more rotten fruit!

Replace negative thought patterns with positive ones that will help combat mental weariness. Make changes to your life physically in order to get more energy. This is a battle that only you can fight. Don't give in to the weariness and belief that this is just the way things are going to be and that you don't have time to take care of yourself. That is exactly what Satan wants you to believe.

There are many ways that busyness can destroy the good fruit in our lives. I believe that *busyness* that results in physical and mental exhaustion has become one of Satan's best tools. Now that you are aware of it, you can change and counter attack the bad-fruit symptoms of busyness!

THE FRUITFUL LIFE

I have great news for you dear friend...you don't have to live your life like a chicken with your head cut off! God can provide you with the right tools to live a busy yet balanced lifestyle. One definition of *balanced* is *the power or ability to decide an outcome by throwing one's strength, influence, support, or the like, to one side or the other.*[8] The power and ability to change into a woman who lives a life that is balanced and healthy belongs only to you. Satan's biggest fear would be that you become an energized woman who starts taking steps toward living a life full of purpose. Satan wants you to fill every moment of your day with unimportant stuff. He loves to watch us collapse in bed at the end of a busy day having done nothing to share Christ's love with others. If he can encourage our weariness, we are no threat to him! On the other hand, the result of using your gifts and talents, reaching out to others and letting Christ shine through you gives Satan a heart attack. As you learn to live a balanced life some of the weariness you have carried around will lighten up. Jesus promises He will lighten your load if we ask. How do we balance out a busy life? We get connected back onto the vine, get nourishment from the source and watch the good fruit grow! Take a closer look at what Jesus said about fruit in our lives:

> "I am the true vine, and my Father is the gardener. He cuts off every branch in me that bears no fruit, while every branch that does bear fruit He prunes so that it will be even more fruitful....Remain in me, and I will remain in you. No branch can bear fruit by itself; it must remain in the vine. Neither can you bear fruit unless you remain in me. I am the vine; you are the branches. If a man remains in me and I in him, he will bear much fruit; apart from me you can do nothing. If anyone does not remain in me, he is like a branch that is thrown away and withers; such branches are picked up, thrown into the fire and burned. If you remain in me and my words remain in you, ask whatever you wish, and it will be given you. This is to my Father's glory, that you bear much fruit, ask whatever you wish, showing yourselves to be my disciples...I have told you this so that my joy may be in you and that your joy may be complete. You did not choose me, but I chose you and appointed you to go and bear fruit–fruit that will last" (John 15:1-11,16).

Jesus often used different metaphors to describe himself such as; He is the bread from heaven or the living water. In John 15, we learn that He is also the "true vine." Our relationship with Jesus is stated in terms of vine and branches–Jesus is the vine, we are the branches and God is the gardener who cares for the branches to make them fruitful. This analogy shows us the importance of remaining in Christ daily. For those of us who learn visually, it is such a great word picture that can be easily understood. As a branch cannot sustain itself without the vine and nourishment it provides, we cannot live a fruitful Christian life without staying connected to Jesus. Fruitful branches are those believers who are connected with Jesus and will "bear much fruit." When we look good, "the gardener" looks good too! When we are not connected and rushing around town like crazy women, our fruit may begin to rot! Or worse, busyness can be the ax that cuts us off from the branch! The vineyard is very precious and costly to God. He paid a great price for His vineyard, which was the precious blood of His Son. He has a great investment in His vineyard and He will take great measures to protect it even if that means disciplining us.

Did you know that the words from Jesus in John 15 are addressed to believers only? Jesus was speaking to the disciples as they walked through the vineyard toward the Mount of Olives and the Garden of Gethsemane only hours before He was arrested and crucified. Of all the conversations He could have had with the disciples knowing He would be leaving this earth shortly, He picked "fruit." It was that important to Him and He wanted to make sure the disciples remembered it. Jesus said in John 15:8, that bearing fruit would be to His Father's glory and would show ourselves as belonging to Him as disciples. God is interested in only one thing–fruit. He is not interested in a pile of dried leaves and branches. Let's take a closer look at the type of fruit Jesus was talking about.

The fruit Jesus referred to in John 15 was not limited to winning souls or starting ministries. Although in Proverbs 11:30 it says "The fruit of the righteous is a tree of life, and he who wins souls is wise." It is God's desire that we win souls, but as John 15 lists–answered prayer, joy and love are also "fruit." In Galatians 5:22–23, we read further of the type of fruit the Spirit produces in us when we abide in Christ. The fruits mentioned here are love, joy, peace, patience, kindness, goodness, faithfulness, gentleness, and self control. As busy women, our lives may only have a few of these traits, but we can change that. Busy women probably struggle the most with patience, especially when we are in a hurry and someone is taking too long! The reality is that a battle wages against our spirit and flesh and the only way to push through that and live a fruitful life is to get connected to the vine. Apart from the vine, we can do nothing just as the Scripture says. We will fight in vain, because it is so unnatural for us to love people we don't even know. Staying connected to the vine is essential in our Christian walk and is hard work!

In the book *Freedom from Busyness*, the author makes a great statement about fruit in our lives. He says, "We go through the motions of our faith but produce no 'fruit,' no significant evidence that we belong to God. It's not that we don't want to bear fruit. Most of us do. Rather, our barrenness is a natural result of busyness. We're so focused on our endless to-do lists that we ignore God. And no God this month means no fruit this month."[9]

Our faith must be more than belief in certain facts; it must result in real growth that is evident by our fruit. We can't let busyness be the hindrance that keeps us from spending time with the Lord. When we put our relationship with God first, we will bear good fruit in our lives.

Again, the major key to bear fruit is to stay connected to the vine. As we learned in previous chapters, the only way we can produce God's quality and quantity of fruit is through an intimate fellowship with the vine. This only happens in daily quiet time with the Lord in prayer and meditation of His Word. Jesus speaks about "remaining in Him," because our fellowship with Him can be interrupted. Jesus knew the distractions of this world would be a problem for His believers (especially busy women).

TAKING CARE OF THE VINEYARD

In John 15:2-3, the subject of pruning is described. Jesus makes two distinctions between two different kinds of pruning: (1) separating and (2) cutting back branches. Fruitful branches are often cut back to promote growth. We have rose bushes my husband cuts back each year in order for them to have an opportunity to grow back even fuller. It is the same with our lives. Sometimes God must discipline us through painful experiences that strengthen our character and faith. Branches that don't bear fruit are cut off at the trunk not only because they are worthless, but they often infect the rest of the tree. If there are any areas in our lives that can contaminate our growth, God will often reveal those to us. These areas could include unforgiveness, bitterness, jealousy, discontentment, gossip, selfish ambition, etc. While the pruning process can be painful at times, it is God's desire for us to grow and flourish into beautiful women of God. Psalm 128:1-2 is a very encouraging verse that I have had on my refrigerator for years. It is a promise that says– "Blessed are all who fear the Lord, who walk in His ways. You will eat the fruit of your labor; blessings and prosperity will be yours."

One of the very real struggles we have as busy women is one that can affect our physical bodies and hinder us from bearing fruit. I'm talking to all the tired women out there. Ask yourself–what kind of fruit do I produce? Is it rotten fruit such as anger, weariness, frustration, hopelessness or depression to name a few? Or would my family say that I am producing good fruit such as patience, love, kindness and slow to anger? What can we do to ward off our weariness? I'm going to tell you one thing that you already know but wish you didn't! How about taking a very proactive approach at overcoming fatigue with exercise or even a nap? Exercise is known to help in the energy department. I admit that I struggle in this area and absolutely hate to exercise (especially at the gym). But I did find that I liked walking if I had a destination to head toward. I also found that it is much more fun to walk if you have a friend. So I formulated an exercise plan to help me gain some more energy during the day. Let me share my idea because you might want to do it too! I got a few friends to join me twice a week and we walk to the local coffee shop! I know what you are thinking. She walks to get a high-calorie drink, doesn't that cancel out her walk? Well, I thought about that for about a minute and decided that since I drink an iced tea every day, why not work to get it twice a week! That is part of my plan to take care of my body. I found something that works best with my schedule and personality. Your exercise plan may look much different than mine depending on your personality. Also, sometimes the best thing you can do for your body is to get some extra rest and take a nap. You have the okay from me to take a nap without feeling guilty! If you aren't getting enough rest, your whole family can suffer. Taking a nap can be the best thing for you and your family.

Another area of our lives that can produce rotten fruit is our negative thought patterns. If you struggle in this area, I would recommend Joyce Meyer's book *Battlefield of the Mind*[10] as a great place to start. How easy it is to let a negative thought enter your mind and let that determine your mood and course for the day. God has opened up my eyes to the revelation that I need to be really careful about what I think about. I heard a speaker recently say, "Don't fight a negative thought, *replace* it!" For example, the more we tell ourselves not to eat the cookies on the counter, the more we want the cookies, right (or maybe that's just me). However, if we tell ourselves, I am going to make myself a sweet healthy snack, if there is such a thing, then we will stop thinking about the cookies and focus on the alternative. It is the same with our thought patterns. If I think all day about how a person offended me, it's going to stir up my emotions, I'm going to get upset and the result is a bad mood. My family then suffers from my dwelling on the negative. When in actuality I have a lot of things to be thankful for and should spend more time meditating on the good to counteract the negative. The truth is that whatever is in our thoughts transfers into our hearts. That's why we need our daily quiet times, because it is there that our thoughts become more centered on God and what is really important in life. We can also become more aware of the enemy's attack on our minds and counteract it with the Word of God. If you don't meditate on the Word of God and spend time with Jesus daily, you won't have any words in your heart to counterattack Satan's schemes. That is why Scripture memorization is so important. Then you can draw from the truth of God's Word when the enemy is trying to penetrate your thought life and emotions.

    I once heard that feelings are a gauge of your thought life. I can bear witness that it has been true in my life. How true it is that whatever you are thinking about can affect your mood. Honestly ladies, our days have a 50/50 chance of going either way (especially if it's that time of month!). Yes we are hormonal, but we don't have to let it dictate our moods. If you struggle in this area, talk to your doctor (we live in the 21st century and there is help out there!). If negativity is a problem for you, begin to change your belief system on the inside to be positive in all situations and your feelings will follow. Whatever you meditate on you will reinforce. So start meditating on the Word of God and stop reinforcing the lies the enemy is feeding you. Don't be naïve, the Bible says that there is a spiritual war waging all around us. Engage in the battle head on by picking up your sword (the Bible) and counteracting the enemy's lies with truth. The Bible says in 2 Corinthians 10:5, "We demolish arguments and every pretension that sets itself up against the knowledge of God, and we take captive every thought to make it obedient to Christ." You have all the power you need to fight the enemy's attack on your mind. Satan is the author of lies and he knows just what to tell you so that you believe it could be true. Take back your thought life and start taking care of yourself. Remember 1 Corinthians 6:19–20, "Do you not know that your body is a temple of the Holy Spirit, who is in you, whom you have received from God? You are not your own; you were bought at a price. Therefore honor God with your body." God says to take care of our bodies because He knew we needed that encouragement. If you do, the weariness will improve.

LET YOUR LIFE SHINE

Matthew 5:14–16 says, *"You are the light of the world. A city on a hill cannot be hidden. Neither do people light a lamp and put it under a bowl. Instead they put it on its stand, and it gives light to everyone in the house. In the same way, let your light shine before men*, that they may see your good deeds and praise your Father in heaven." As you begin to take care of yourself (body, mind and spirit), your light will shine brighter and you will become a more effective witness. Have you ever tried walking with a lit candle? Better yet, think about how slow you have to walk with a birthday cake ablaze with candles? You have to walk *slowly* because the candle will flicker and sometimes go out. It is the same way with your life and the light you are carrying. God wants us to carry the light of His presence with us, but if we go too fast we can lose it. Don't let busyness choke out the flame that God is asking you to carry. You need to protect your time with Him and your thought life, so you are prepared to minister to any people that God brings across your path. Take Timothy's words to heart as he writes in 2 Timothy 1:6–7 "For this reason I remind you to fan into flame the gift of God, which is in you through the laying on of my hands. For God did not give us a spirit of timidity, but a spirit of power, of love and of self-discipline." Start today disciplining your body and thoughts against weariness. You can transform your tired weary self into a powerful woman of God who is capable of fighting Satan's schemes that distract you from your real purpose. Today is a great day to regain your strength and stamina for the battle ahead!

OUR HEART'S RESPONSE

Read Matthew 7:16–20

1. What is one way to recognize a believer based on these verses?

2. What type of fruit do you currently produce? What does it look like?

3. If you are struggling in some of the areas of rotten fruit (weariness, moodiness, etc.) how can you make changes to overcome it?

Read Matthew 12:33

4. What promises are made in this verse when a tree is made good or bad? How do you change a tree?

5. A life source makes all the difference on what type of fruit you will produce. What is your life source, or where do you go when you are stressed? Is it the Lord or something else (friends, television, the Internet, food, etc.)?

7

HIS HEART...

She Would Influence the Next Generation for Christ

*Point your kids in the right direction—when they
are old they won't be lost.*
Proverbs 22:6 (THE MESSAGE)

It is God's heart for this generation of busy moms to rise up in these last days and engage in the battle for our children and grandchildren's salvation. Unfortunately, we live in a pagan society where Christian morals are not the majority anymore. The message that the world is trying to teach our kids is that almost anything goes as long as you are happy. The media has done a pretty good job of introducing shows to our children that contain witchcraft, sexuality, disrespectful kids, and often devalue the family unit. This has become one of Satan's subtle tools to steer our children away from the Christian values we teach them. Many parents in this generation have forgotten that the most important job we have is *passing the baton of faith from one generation to*

another. James Dobson once put it this way–he likened the mission of introducing one's children to the Christian faith to a three-man relay race. "First," he says, "your father runs his lap around the track, carrying the baton, which represents the gospel of Jesus Christ. At the appropriate moment, he hands the baton to you, and you begin your journey around the track. Then finally, the time will come when you must get the baton safely in the hands of your child. But as any track coach will testify: *RELAY RACES ARE WON OR LOST IN THE TRANSFER OF THE BATON.* There is a critical moment when all can be lost by a fumble or miscalculation. The baton is rarely dropped on the back side of the track when the runner has it firmly in his grasp. If failure is to occur, it will likely happen in the exchange between generations!"[11] How good of an athlete or student our child has become is not how we should measure the success of our parenting, but rather did we raise up our children to be godly men and women who would not be swayed by the world.

Unfortunately, this generation may fail to pass on the baton of Christianity successfully. There are studies that have been done on our generation that show an alarming decline in the commitment to Christianity compared to previous generations. Moms, specifically, are less likely to share their faith with others, get involved in church or even consider their faith as a very important part of their life. Moms of my generation are also less likely to volunteer in church, read their Bible or even attend church on a regular basis. If we continue on this path, our nation's moral character will be compromised and future generations will be in trouble. However, if we take a stand today, we can make a difference. Moms have connections with each other that can be a tool in leading other mothers to the Lord. When a busy mom reaches out and encourages another mom to take her children to church, a generation has just been changed. Women are the most open to hearing about the Lord during motherhood than any other time in their lives. A mom knows instinctively when her newborn baby is placed in her arms that she will have the single greatest influence on that child. The most important gift you can give your children is raising them to know and love Jesus Christ as their personal Savior.

WELCOME TO MOTHERHOOD!

Do you remember the day you became a mother? I imagine that you are like me and can remember the exact moment you held your child for the first time. It was an overwhelming rush of feelings of joy, love, and excitement. God had actually trusted you with a human life to love and be responsible for. And what a responsibility that turned out to be! Not only were you responsible for your child's health, safety and well being, but you knew instinctively that you also had the tremendous responsibility of raising your child to love and respect the Lord.

I could hardly wait to become a mother! I was 19 years old when I married my husband, but don't tell my daughter because she can't get married until she's 30! We decided to wait to start our family until he finished college. I worked full-time for the first five years of marriage and helped to put Mike through school. Since I was so anxious to start my family it was especially hard to see so many of my friends at church get pregnant, even though I was young and had plenty of time. At one point, I remember being one of the only girls in my Young Marrieds' group who wasn't pregnant and how lonely that felt. I actually cried about not having a baby one Mother's Day. I have to laugh now, because I had no idea what I was getting myself into, and that I would actually cry more often *after* I had kids! I was working full-time, and was never around these new moms except on Sunday (when those babies always seemed to look their cutest). I missed all the casual conversations that would have clued me in to how exhausting and overwhelming motherhood really is. I entered motherhood unprepared for how hard (but rewarding) it would turn out to be. When I did become a mother, I had an instant connection with all my friends who were also mothers (let alone every other mom on earth), and that was a great feeling.

THE MOTHERHOOD CONNECTION

It's true: moms all over the world share a special connection with each other that is unlike any other relationship on earth. We can share labor stories with all the details and not blush. We can have fun comparing stories on whether or not we had an epidural and how long we lasted until we got it, or even better, share that we gave birth naturally without any medication! Personally, I requested an epidural from my doctor when I was around seven months' pregnant. I made sure my doctor made a note in my chart.

The connection between mothers can be felt in their instinct to look after each other's children in any given situation. I recently had a friend share with me how her daughter got lost in a crowd. The little girl remembered that her mom told her to find another mommy with kids if she ever got lost. My friend instinctively knew that a mom would not let a lost child out of her sight until her parents were found. This is so true. She found her daughter minutes later with a mom who was not going to budge until the little girl's parents were found. Moms look out for each other. When my friend Kim was murdered, one of her closest friends stepped in to take care of her daughter during the transition time before she was adopted by a family member. She referred to this as a "labor of love."

Moms are always on the go because we have so many family responsibilities to take care of. We love time-savers such as a drive-thru anything! I love to drive through my local coffee store for my caffeine fix. Did I mention I *love* drive-thru car washes? Not only are the kids contained in the car, they're entertained while watching the soap and brushes clean the car. I personally like to pretend to roll down the window when the air dryer is on and watch my youngest hit the floor in fear of getting sucked out! (I know it sounds mean, but it makes the rest of us laugh). The kids don't even realize that all this excitement just saved mom from having to sit on a bench and wait for the car to be done while they play with the ash trays and in bushes. Is it just my kids or do yours do the same thing? On the topic of being on the go, I'm probably one of the fastest shoppers in town. I can go to the bank, grocery store, post office and grab an iced tea in less than an hour. I recently realized how fast I really am (and was a little embarrassed) when a close friend of mine said, "I always see you at the store, but you are shopping so fast, I can't catch up with you to say hi." It's true. I do shop really fast, but the Lord has convicted me to slow down and be aware of His promptings to reach out during this mad rush. Along the way I have had more and more opportunities to meet and minister to people. I've even been prompted by the Holy Spirit to pray for a few people while I was buying that much-needed iced tea at the coffee store.

    Another connection moms share is their sense of humor. We can relate to and laugh at each other's mistakes. Let's face it; you really do need to have a sense of humor to keep from going crazy. Let me tell you a story that will make you laugh. One hot summer day, I was taking my oldest son Austin to swim lessons. I was, as usual, running late when I left the house in a whirlwind of commotion. I loaded up the "A" Team in all their car seats which, as you know, is a job by itself. On the way, I was going to stop at the local pool supply store to buy a pair of goggles for my son (who would not swim without them!). I can still remember jumping out of the car and realizing that something felt really hot on my feet.

I looked down and to my horror and disbelief, I had forgotten my shoes! In that moment, I had a decision to make…do I go home for my shoes or go in? I was running late and didn't see a "no shoes, no shirt, no service" sign, so I went into the pool store apologizing the whole time. I was so embarrassed, but still manage to laugh at myself today. I can also laugh at the time I came out of the bathroom of a Southern California theme park with a strip of toilet paper hanging out of the back of my pants. My husband spotted it and was horrified. I had recently given birth to my youngest son Aaron, with a room full of strangers. (I *think* they worked at the hospital!) So toilet paper hanging out of my pants didn't even begin to make me blush. As moms, we learn to laugh at ourselves and take things in stride (thank God for our sense of humor).

MOTHERHOOD GUILT

However, moms also share another connection which is not so funny–motherhood guilt. There probably isn't a mother on earth who hasn't experienced this feeling at some point. We tend to take everything we do wrong to heart and are positive we have damaged our kids for life. I wasn't really anticipating how much this would become a part of my life when I first became a mom. Remember, I wasn't in on mom conversations until *after* I had our baby. I really thought I had what it took to be the best mom ever. I thought I was a patient person because I rarely got mad at my husband. I had the misconception that I would stay the same person when I had kids! I learned quickly that when you are pushed just the right way, you become that person you never knew you were. I remember daydreams about having cute little kids who would let me hug and kiss them all day, and all the fun things we would do together. I never thought I would struggle with motherhood guilt because I was going to do everything exactly right. (Believe me, reading a book about babies and taking care of one are two different things!) I felt guilty just three days after bringing my firstborn, Austin, home from the hospital! I remember taking him to the Hospital Well Baby Care Center to have him checked out a few days after we brought him home from the hospital. I had him dressed in a gown that had the drawstring and flaps that you could cover their hands with (you know, so they won't scratch themselves). I had covered his hands in the flaps from the first day he came home (my mom told me I needed to do this). The first thing the nurse said was, "Uncover those hands...he needs his hands...you are going to stunt his development." We actually laughed about it later on saying that he was three days behind all the other babies because we had covered his hands. Initially, I felt like I had blown it. Has anyone else ever accidentally given their kids too much cold medicine? I have. How about watching your baby roll off the bed and land on his back, or worse his head? Been there, done that at least once with each of my three kids (you would think I would have learned the first time it happened)! When your kids get older, motherhood guilt continues to come and go with each new stage of life. I recently almost had a panic attack realizing that my oldest son would be 18 before I knew it and I wondered if we had taught him enough Christian values. Where does the time go?

While other people roll their eyes at a screaming child whose mom is trying to load him up in the car, mothers understand the frustration. The mom connection can be felt by any mother on earth because no matter what our children's ages are, we have all been there at one time or another. This connection is key to reach out and share Christ's love and compassion, especially from one mother to another.

A MOTHER'S OPEN HEART

There is a tremendous open window of opportunity for a busy mom to share her faith with another mom during this incredibly hectic time of raising young kids. I have found that most moms I have established a relationship with will be open to hearing about my church and faith. Also, a busy mom has the most opportunities to meet people and share Christ's love and compassion during this season of life. As I said in previous chapters, think about how many kids you have and multiply all the activities each one is in throughout the year. These are the amount of harvest fields that Jesus was speaking about in the book of Matthew. There are potentially hundreds of moms that you can meet during a one-year period. The many connections you share with these moms represent a huge advantage in cultivating friendships that can lead to sharing your faith and Christ's love and compassion in tangible ways. There is nothing more refreshing for a busy mom than to be encouraged by another mom who can actually relate to what she is experiencing. There are a lot of moms who feel like they are the only ones struggling. These moms just need to be reassured that they aren't alone.

Most women that I meet in the community usually have some kind of religious upbringing, but may not be a member of a church. Maybe they left the church when the decision became their own to go or not. Remember, your children will also have to make the decision on their own to follow Christ when they are adults. I have found that an interesting phenomenon begins to happen when a woman becomes a mother. Something is stirred up inside of her that brings the realization that she is responsible for the spiritual upbringing of her new child. She may not have even given it much thought before the child was born. I believe that the Holy Spirit stirs the mother's heart to realize the opportunity she has to influence her child spiritually. This is a defining moment in a new mother's life when she is the most open to pursue a relationship with the Lord. She will consider taking her children to church even if her husband will not go with her. I call this an open window of opportunity. You could very well be the friend God has put into her life who points her to Jesus and a great church to take her children to.

Opportunities to meet new people in public places have become a little bit more challenging these days. With almost everyone owning a cell phone, it becomes easier to shut the world out and just talk to whomever you choose. Parks are great places to make new friends. When I took my children to the park, I always looked for opportunities to meet new moms and let the Lord lead me to reach out in a particular area. I often invited moms I would meet to join the MOMS Club®. Starting conversations with other moms is very easy, just talk about the kids.

I once had God prompt me to reach out to a mom at a fast food restaurant. My Bible study group at the time was doing a study on raising boys. I noticed that she had two young boys and one reminded me of Aaron, my youngest. I felt led to invite her to our group. I got up from the table and introduced myself and started talking to her about her son who at that moment was trying to escape out of the high chair. I started to tell her about my group and she said that she had just finished reading the book that went with the study. Wow, I thought, what is the coincidence of that? She then told me that she just moved here from out of state that same week. She was excited to receive the invitation. We exchanged phone numbers and she began coming to my Bible study. She was a Christian, but as she began to come to our group, a hunger for a more intimate relationship with Jesus stirred in her. Instantly, she made a whole new group of friends, which normally would have taken a long time since she didn't know anyone in the area when she moved. She became one of my closest friends and it was exciting to watch her relationship grow with the Lord during that season.

Another time God prompted me to reach out to a mom was when I took a bike ride to the park with my youngest son, Aaron. I had written an evangelistic booklet and had a strong desire to start passing it out. As you can imagine, this involves boldness, which is not natural for me (or for most people). The Holy Spirit prompted me to take a booklet with me just in case I saw an opportunity. When we arrived, I started talking to a mom whose son was playing with mine. We talked about babysitters and she shared with me that she didn't have anyone to watch her son. I realized that this was an ideal opportunity. I asked her if she attended a church. She looked a little surprised that I was so forward. She quickly said she went to a church nearby. I then turned it around and told her that sometimes churches have lists of babysitters and that she should check with her church. The conversation then turned into her sharing with me that she was going to this particular church because her mother-in-law went there and although she didn't like it, it would just devastate her mother-in-law if she and her husband left. She admitted that she wasn't getting anything out of the services, but had to wait until her mother-in-law was basically dead until they considered changing denominations! I felt led to give her one of the booklets and told her that it really wasn't about her mother-in-law, but the spiritual upbringing of her son. She needed to put him first and find a church she felt comfortable in. She lit up and asked me if I came to this park often so we could meet again and we exchanged phone numbers. I know that seeds were planted in her by our brief conversation that day.

RELATIONSHIP IS KEY

I want you to recognize that there is a difference between simply handing her a booklet about the Lord and taking the time to get to know her first. If I had just randomly handed her the booklet, she probably would have thrown it away before she left the park. Once we had established a connection, even in those brief moments, she could see that I was genuinely interested in helping her. There is a profound saying, *People don't care about what you know until they know you care.* People can tell if you're truly interested in them or not. When you take the time to build a relationship, even for a few minutes, people are generally more receptive to hear your words of encouragement or offer to help. Building a relationship could happen in just a few minutes or a few months, it depends on the situation. Listen to the Lord and determine what He prompts you to do.

I recently heard about a soccer mom who had the reputation of being a born-again Christian. Not many coaches wanted her child on their team. A friend of mine heard that she was going to have this child on her soccer team and was really nervous about it. Apparently this mom had a very strong personality and would try to save people during games and practices. Understandably, this made the other parents on the team uncomfortable. I cannot express enough that relationship is key in sharing with other people and having them receive what you say. In a twist, this particular mom's pushy tactics actually helped in opening the window of opportunity for me to share with my friend when she asked me, "What is a born-again Christian?"

Be deliberate about meeting other moms during your child's activities, but don't overdo it. Instead of reading a book at the next activity you attend, talk to a mom nearby. Most moms will open up if they sense you care and are listening. See if the Lord has opened the heart of another mom during the next practice you attend. When you become more available, the Lord will send people your way. He may use you once a week, once a month or once in awhile. The important thing is to be alert to what people say around you and be sensitive to the opportunities God orchestrates. God recently spoke to me and told me that there were hurting people all around me, but they were going to be hard to identify. He told me to listen to their conversations and He would give me the words to say at the right moment. Remember, people may hide behind a mask, but God can see through it. He feels their pain. Be ready because He will send these people to you as you become more available and more aware.

OUR HEART'S RESPONSE

Read Deuteronomy 6:5-9

1. What is your responsibility as a mom, based on these verses?

2. Are you taking an active role in teaching your children about God? Or are you relying on your church alone to teach them?

3. If you want your children to follow God, you must make God a part of your everyday experiences. In what ways can you do that despite your busy schedule?

4. Are there any moms in your life right now that you have established a relationship with and can invite to church or a Bible study?

    a. If you don't reach out to those moms, who else do you think will?

8

The Struggles of *Her Heart*

*The Lord will fulfill His purpose for me;
Your love, O Lord, endures forever—Do not
abandon the works of your hands.*
Psalm 138:8

We have come to the end of our journey of discovering God's heart for your life as a busy woman. I hope that you will embrace life with a new confidence to become a woman God can use to impact others for Him. You are equipped to impact this generation for Christ as soon as you get enough courage to step out in faith. Even though I am writing this book, I still struggle with living out my own outreach ministry each day. I know it is hard and requires us to step out of our normal comfort zone. I'm a busy woman myself and I know that our natural default can be just get through the day. This falls right into Satan's plan for living a life without purpose and I want you to take steps to break out of this cycle today! It is the complete opposite of the purpose of God's heart for us. Satan is the master of distractions. He will do anything to keep our focus off of Jesus and onto ourselves and our busy circumstances. With the help of the Lord, we can become busy women focused on the goal of impacting lives during the course of this busy season of life. I would like to share a few more struggles that can keep you from beginning the journey of fulfilling the purposes of God's heart for your life.

"COMFORTABLE" IS A DANGEROUS PLACE

One thing that I have learned is that God is not okay with me staying in an infant stage of Christianity. As we accept Jesus as our personal Lord and Savior, we are considered babes. 1 Peter 2:2 says it this way–"Like newborn babies, crave pure spiritual milk, so that by it you may grow up in your salvation." We go to church weekly, study the Bible, fellowship with other believers and pray, we should start to "crave pure spiritual milk." When we give in to this craving for more of God's Word and feed ourselves, we begin to grow. We can't rely solely on our pastor to feed us once a week on Sunday mornings. It isn't enough nourishment for the whole week. Keep in mind, this craving can be replaced with something else if we aren't careful (remember the Snickers story). I was stuck in a non-growth mode for years. God occasionally impressed upon me to spend more time with Him, but I told Him I didn't have time. Only He knew about those stubborn years. If you continue to ignore that impression, sometimes God will stop asking. That is a scary place to be, because then it is all up to you to initiate the relationship again. We can go years without even thinking about it and drift away from Him all together. While I ignored the prompting to spend more time with Jesus, I looked like I had it together. I even led a Bible study group. On the inside I knew I wasn't living the way God intended for me. I also knew He had bigger plans for my life that weren't going to happen until I matured more spiritually. Our walk with the Lord is developed and matured in different stages, but we should constantly strive to grow. The benefit of growing in our faith is that the more mature we become, the deeper things God can reveal to you. You do not arrive one day fully mature, instead it is a process you go through your whole entire life.

Please don't settle for a Christian life that is comfortable. You will limit God on how much He can trust and use you if you never mature. The Message Bible puts it this way in Ephesians 4, "No prolonged infancies among us, please. We'll not tolerate babes in the woods, small children who are an easy mark for impostors. God wants us to grow up, to know the whole truth and tell it in love–like Christ in everything." It is a dangerous place to remain as a baby Christian. Not only are you a target for Satan to feed you lies, but if faced with a crisis, you may not have the foundation to get through a tough situation. It took the major crisis of losing a friend to get me more serious about my relationship with the Lord. Strive to become mature now! The more mature you are, the more impact you will have on the lives of your family members. Chances are that your children will not mature any further than the stage you have reached. It is close to impossible for them to grow at a faster rate than you when they are children. You are to be a living example that assists in the development of your own children becoming mature Christian believers one day. How can you lead by example if you don't even know the Bible well enough to share with your kids or have enough faith to pray for areas of need in your life? Ladies, this will only happen if you spend time at Jesus' feet in quiet meditation of the Word and prayer. The Bible becomes your spiritual food that you cannot live without. His presence becomes the very air you breathe!

GIVE HIM MORE OF YOU

Another important lesson that God taught me was that He desires not only more of my time but *more of me*. One day while I was worshipping the Lord in church, we were singing a song about wanting *more of Jesus* in our lives. While I was singing, the Lord began to speak to my heart that it was His desire that I give Him more of me! I think as Christians we do want more of God in our lives. In actuality it is His same desire to have more areas of our lives available to Him to do His work. It is easy to sing songs that are full of intentions to be available to God, but are those really true? Sometimes we only give Him a part of ourselves. What God said to me that day was, "When you only give me one leg, how can you walk to where I am leading? If you give me only one ear, how can you fully hear my voice? If you only give me one hand, how can you receive what I am depositing into one hand to be given out with the other? One of any body part is not as effective as the whole body dedicated to fulfilling my directions to reach out. I would rather you give me all, than just a part of who you are. If you are only willing to give me just one part of yourself, don't bother until you are willing to give it all." If we each decided to give all of ourselves to God, we can impact this generation for Christ! Ask yourself how much you are really giving of yourself to God. Are you holding anything back?

REALIZE THAT EACH DAY IS A GIFT

The other important lesson God showed me was that each day on this earth is really a *gift* from God. You cannot go back and redeem yesterdays. None of us knows when our last day on earth will be. Each day is not only a gift from God, but an opportunity to thank Him for that day by being available as He directs. In fact, we will all give an account on how we lived our lives on judgment day. Since He is the one who gives us the gift of life, the least we can do is make Him look good during the course of our day. We make Him look good when we live upright and reach out to others. We can sometimes let our days be filled with things that aren't that important in the grand scheme of life. God does want us to enjoy life, but not at the expense of stealing time away from Him or the work He is calling us to. When we get caught up in shopping, the Internet, social outings, phone calls, etc., we can waste hours of valuable time. God has really convicted me in this area of being a good steward of my time. I try to plan my days accordingly. We all need occasional "me" time and that's okay. However, when it interferes with what God is calling you to do, it can become a distraction. I would encourage you to figure out where some of those time wasters are and replace them with what God tells you to do. You will be amazed at what can be cut out of your life and how much time you can redeem back. You can do what you really want to do.

YOU CAN DO IT!

It is God's desire that He exceed your highest expectations for your life. Don't just settle for the status quo! It is not God's nature to do things in an ordinary way. Just read through the Old Testament, God used ordinary people to do extraordinary things! If God can take an ordinary Israelite woman named Esther and place her on the throne as a queen who ultimately saved the lives of her people–He can do anything! We need to learn to dream bigger dreams for our lives. God can do amazing things through lives that are available to carry forth the plans that God created them to do. I would have never thought that writing a book was part of God's plan for my life. Yet, I knew it was His idea and plan for me to write the message that was placed in my heart and nothing could hold me back. Yes, it took a while to get the message written and there were many obstacles along the way, but I knew I could not give up. God's timing turned out to be perfect.

You too can achieve any dreams that God has placed on your heart. Some of the dreams God may have given you in the past can still come into fulfillment as you stay committed to Him and trust His timing. Whatever God is calling you to, do your homework, make a plan and go for it! The Message Bible says in Ephesians 3, "God can do anything, you know—far more than you could ever imagine or guess or request in your wildest dreams! He does it not by pushing us around but by working within us, His spirit deeply and gently within us." Jesus is the perfect gentlemen who will not force you to do anything you are not ready to do. Sometimes it can be a long process to get us to where He wants us to go. Regardless of how old you are, it's never too late to make a difference in someone's life. Some of your gifts, talents and dreams may have become dormant, but it's not too late! Start getting connected back to the vine and let God breathe new life into your very soul. With God's help, you can do anything that you set your mind to!

Now go ahead and impact the world for Christ—one life at a time!

APPENDIX A

Ideas for Using Your Spiritual Gifts and Natural Talents for Outreach

According to 1 Peter 4:10, *"Each one should use whatever gift he has received to serve others."* We have discussed throughout the book that God has given each person spiritual gifts and natural talents that can be used to bless others in many different ways. While each gift and talent can be categorized into a main area, they can be demonstrated in many ways depending on the needs of your community. For example, the gift of serving can be demonstrated from serving meals in a homeless shelter to serving your child's teacher as a helper in the classroom. While they are given differently, both spiritual gifts and natural talents are listed together in this section. Some of the spiritual gifts listed which I believe are given to only Christians are apostleship, evangelism, discernment, faith, pastoral, prayer, prophetic and wisdom. The natural talents listed were given at birth when God created you and may have been tapped into as early as childhood or at any time during your life. The amazing thing is that both spiritual gifts and natural talents can operate together in effective ways for outreach to others. Remember, as you use your gifts and talents to bless others you are sowing seeds into the lives of others that will hopefully draw them into a relationship with Christ.

The following is only a partial list of gifts and talents, together with specific ideas for using each one in outreach. This list is meant to assist you in discovering what your own abilities are and give you ideas about how you can use them to bless others. These outreach ideas are meant to inspire you with more ideas to incorporate into your community. Pray that God will show you the areas He has gifted you in and that He will inspire you with new ideas to bless others for him.

GIFTS AND TALENTS

ADMINISTRATION: Organize, supervise or take charge of events or groups; bringing ideas and details together are your strength; you know how to take an idea and follow through with the steps to make it happen; you enjoy the planning and organizing stages of events the most.

Ideas: Organize a group of people who have the same interests or hobbies as you and meet on a regular basis. Playing Bunco, scrapbooking and a girl's night out are great monthly ideas for women. I once started a Bunco group for moms at school who met monthly. We discovered that most of the women were Christians as the topic of women's Bible studies came up often in our conversation. I felt God leading me to start a group using these women as the core group. We invited others at school and the group is still meeting almost four years later. This has become my ministry at the school. I am always looking for more women to invite who are searching. If you want to start a group, you don't have to be a teacher, but rather a facilitator of the group. You can buy a topical book or Bible study and be the facilitator of the discussion time. If you don't feel led to start a Bible study group, you can still look for opportunities to reach out during your fun nights together. It's all about building relationship and looking for opportunities to demonstrate Christ's love and compassion. Also, consider offering your organizational skills to someone who could use some organizing in their life. Organizing really is a gift and very few people have it!

APOSTLESHIP: Start and lead new ministries that advance the kingdom; you love a challenge especially when what you are starting has never been done before; you are not afraid to work hard to go from vision to ministry.

Ideas: Once you have identified what you are most passionate about and what areas you are gifted in, think of a way that you can start a ministry doing just that. It can be anything from helping widows, children, elderly or young people. You can show them God's love and compassion by meeting their immediate needs. Study your community and pray about what the needs are. God will give you ideas if you seek His counsel.

ATHLETIC: Physically active; loves outdoor activities; you don't mind a little friendly competition or sweat; you are physically disciplined and take good care of yourself.

Ideas: When you work out at the gym, ask God to highlight someone for you to start a conversation with. If you are good at personal training, offer to meet someone at the gym on a regular basis who is trying to get in shape. The best conversations happen during workouts. Organize a group of ladies to walk together each week. Start a neighborhood sporting event such as kickball, soccer or baseball. Invite families to play once a month at a local schoolyard. You can also join a recreational team sport in your community. These are harvest fields to meet people you normally may not. If you have children, consider being an assistant or coach of their team sport. This is another way to get to know people in your community.

ARTISTIC: Gifted in many ways relating to art that can include painting, drawing, crafts, and decorating to name a few; your creations express God's love in ways that words cannot; you are often inspired to create something new and different with your hands.

Ideas: Donate artwork or crafts that you created to various events or causes. For example, if your child's school is having a fundraiser, donate any item you made to help raise money for the school. If your creation has a religious meaning or inspiration, don't be afraid to share it with others. This can be a great witnessing tool done in a natural way. Another practical idea is to teach an art or drawing class in the summer for kids at a discounted price. You can also offer to paint a mural at a children's hospital, library, or home of someone who normally could not afford such a luxury. These are all ways to meet new people and bless them with your talents. If you are good at decorating, offer to shop with a friend who needs ideas for their home.

COOKING: Find enjoyment and fulfillment preparing meals for the ones you love; you are creative with knowing what foods to use for the best tasting dishes; people get excited when they hear you are cooking them a meal.

Ideas: Be aware of opportunities to help cook a meal for someone in need. Delivering a hot meal to a family going through a difficult time lifts the burden for them of figuring out what's for dinner and blesses them tremendously. If you hear that someone is either sick, having surgery, or experiencing a death in the family, these are your opportunities to offer your service. Also, starting a cooking team at church, work, or your child's school is a great idea. If it is at your child's school, it can be run out of the PTA committee. It provides a central place where people can inform you of the need for meals. Start with an announcement or flyer that you are creating a list of people willing to cook. Next make sure everyone knows who the contact person is for scheduling days. (It doesn't have to be you, but someone you know who is good at organizing.) When you personally cook a meal, always offer words of encouragement and let the family know that you are praying for them. If they seem open to it, invite them to your church or Bible study (but be sensitive). If you start this kind of a group, the benefit for ministry is that you will be one of the first people to know if a family is experiencing a crisis. You can offer your assistance in a tangible way by providing a meal and spiritually through offering prayer support.

DISCERNMENT: The ability to recognize truth regardless of the surrounding circumstances; natural insight into the root of the issue; you posses a keen insight in recognizing the intention of others whether it is good or bad.

Ideas: The best use of your gift of discernment is to stay closely connected to God so you can clearly hear His voice. Your ability to speak the truth in love into the lives of others as God directs is very important. Being sensitive to how others will accept your discernment is crucial. The more you discern things in people's lives, the more they will share with you. Words of discernment to an unbeliever can be a life-changing experience for them as you speak God's heart. Ask God for opportunities during your day to minister to others with words of discernment into personal situations.

ENCOURAGEMENT: You can find just the right words to encourage others in times of need; your words of praise or comfort demonstrate love and support to others perfectly; you know just what another person needs to hear and you say it.

Ideas: You are, in essence, a cheerleader in the lives of the people around you. The way that you communicate encouraging words is phenomenal. Your gift operates best in the lives of people who know you personally because they know you are genuine. If you are out and someone you don't know opens up about a personal situation, don't be afraid to offer words of encouragement. There are people in the world who don't have an encouraging friend like you and your words can impact them tremendously. Also, set aside time each week to call your friends to check in and see how they are doing. Occasionally send a card or email to your pastor, friends, and children's teachers to praise them for a job well done. Your gift is in the positive words you write and say to others.

EVANGELISM: Sharing the love of Jesus with others is your passion; your heart grieves as you see unbelievers broken and in need of a Savior; you love to introduce others to Jesus; you try to find creative ways to reach out to others with the gospel.

Ideas: According to Ephesians 4:2 your job as an evangelist is to "prepare God's people for works of service, so that the body of Christ may be built up." Your gift of evangelism is one in which you have natural insight in knowing how to reach out to others with the message of Christ. Your gift is not just for you, but rather a gift that is to be used to equip the body of Christ for outreach. You may also have the gift of teaching which operates well with this gift. Ask God to give you new outreach ideas. I once organized an outreach in the local movie theater. We reached thousands with the gospel when *The Passion of the Christ* movie was in theaters. It was definitely not me, but rather God's idea. Your job as an evangelist is to share any ideas God has given you regarding outreach with the body of Christ. One idea for your gift is to teach a class at church on how to incorporate outreach as a lifestyle. Another idea is to organize a group from church to go out and meet people in the marketplace and share the gospel. Also, consider starting an outreach ministry at your church if you don't already have one.

FAITH: Confidence to boldly come before the Lord on behalf of others through prayer is your strength; you believe that God's hands move when you ask and you pray about everything; the gifts of faith and prayer often operate together which results in a powerful prayer warrior to be reckoned with!

Ideas: Your enthusiasm for the power of prayer is contagious! Look for opportunities to share stories on how God has answered your many prayers. Don't worry if your audience is Christian or not, your experiences will impact all who hear. Don't be afraid to pray for the terminally ill. Offer to go to the hospital and pray for the sick as much as possible.

FRIENDSHIP: Friends are one of the most important things in your life; you get excited about making new friends and always have room for one more; you treat your friends like family and hang out with them often; you are a loyal friend who will stand by your friends through the good and bad times.

Ideas: Always be on the lookout for potential new friends. Carry a card with your phone number on it in case God brings any lonely women to you during your day. If you meet someone, offer to meet them for coffee on a later date. Also, you can be the welcome wagon to new people in your neighborhood. When someone moves in, take them a plate of cookies and introduce yourself. Organize a girl's night out for your friends and encourage them to invite a friend. During your night out you can look for opportunities to invite someone to church or a Bible study. It's important to not just be close friends with people at church, but rather widen your circle of friends to include those who are not exactly like you. If you don't have any non-Christian friends, go find some.

HELPING: Contributing to the needs of others is where you find the most fulfillment; you are good at many trades and love to offer your help wherever it is needed the most;

your goal in life is to make things easier on others; when others need something they think of you; you help others regardless of recognition.

Ideas: When others need help, they think of you. Your heart and willingness to help is a true gift. Since you are good at many things, you can help in almost any capacity. Pray that God shows you exactly where to help and when to hold back so that you only do what He calls you to do. It is easy to get burned out with your gift if you do too much. Look for opportunities to help people in your neighborhood. Offering to help in practical ways speaks volumes to people. There are some routine things that are hard for the elderly or sick to do. Pray that God shows you the needs of your neighborhood and offer to help however God directs.

HOSPITALITY: Your amazing gift provides a warm and welcoming environment for your guests; others feel valued and cared for in your home; the extra things you do while caring for the basic needs of your guests make them feel loved; you throw great parties!

Ideas: Make your home available to host gatherings as needed by your church or friends. Host a luncheon for your friends around Mother's Day and invite some moms you would like to know better. Another nice idea would be to host a tea party at a convalescent home. There are a lot of lonely people there. Throw parties for birthdays as often as you can. Just think how loved someone would feel if you threw them a small surprise party, regardless of how close you were. Just cake, coffee and a few friends would be a great way to celebrate another's birthday. Invite a lonely or hurting woman you know over for tea and make her feel loved. Help your church put on a luncheon by sharing your expertise on how to make the afternoon special.

LEADERSHIP: The ability to lead others with a specific vision or goal in mind; you can direct and encourage others to be the best that they can be; you have insight into the needs of a group and know how to guide them in the right direction; you influence others by your example.

Ideas: Figure out what you are the most passionate about and lead a group of like-minded people with the same goal in mind to make a difference in this world. If you are passionate about moms, start a Bible study for moms in your community. If you love kids, volunteer to lead a group of kids at church or start a neighborhood vacation Bible school in the summer. If you are passionate about new believers, start a new believers' class either in your home or church. Offer to use your gift of leadership for projects at work or school. People watch how you lead and will be drawn to the Lord by your example.

MUSICIAN: Plays a musical instrument well; you may also have a beautiful singing voice; you see music as an escape from the stresses of the world; you find great fulfillment in creating beautiful melodies either in song or instrument.

Ideas: If you haven't already done so, join other musicians at your church in leading worship. Research the various venues where you can share your musical talent in the marketplace. Don't believe that you are limited to use your musical gift only in church. There are many public places where musicians can play. You will have to research where these places are in your community. Also, you could teach an instrument or vocal class for students for free or at a discounted price. Volunteer to teach children music at your church. If you don't have a children's choir, start one. Find out about any musicals being produced in your community and try out. This is also another way to meet people.

PASTORAL: You posses the deep desire to take spiritual responsibility for a group of people; taking care of and nurturing people's spiritual lives are your passion; you are really a shepherd of the flock of believers; you have a way about you that draws people into sharing deep things in their lives because they feel that you really do care.

Ideas: First of all, realize that this is a gift that isn't solely for Pastors of churches. A pastoral gift is recognized most in someone who really loves and cares about the people in their life. People with a pastoral heart can use their gift not only at church but in the workplace or community. The more you take a genuine interest in the lives of others the more they will think about coming to you when they have a problem. When you are available to listen to people who are having issues and offer them support–you are sowing seeds that God uses to draw others to him. Being able to trust you with what is going on in their lives is huge because it is hard to find people you can trust these days. When people open up with you (which is really easy to do), pray that God gives you words of encouragement for their situation. Your goal as a shepherd is to be on the lookout for the lost sheep of the world and gently guide them in the direction of Christ.

PRAYER: Offering up prayers to the Lord daily comes very natural to you; you have devoted your life to petitions, praise, and thanksgiving to the Lord on all occasions; others ask you to pray for them often because they know you will; you may be involved in prayer ministry at your church.

Ideas: Be disciplined to pray on all occasions for all kinds of requests. Also, when you meet a stranger who shares a need, offer to pray for them on the spot. If you hear of someone in the hospital, offer to go and pray even if you don't know them personally. Start a mobile prayer team at your church that will go and pray for anyone who needs immediate prayer. Begin a prayer group at your child's school that meets with other moms and prays for the teachers, staff, and students. Pray for the leaders in your own church and others you know in ministry. Devote your life to being a prayer warrior!

PROPHETIC: God speaks His heart to you often for His people; you know how to publically communicate God's Word; the messages you deliver from God offers believers comfort, encouragement, guidance and warning; you can be viewed as God's mouthpiece.

Ideas: Your gift is very powerful as you speak God's heart into situations. You must operate in this gift with clarity of hearing what the Lord is saying in any situation. Your gift edifies the body of believers, but don't be afraid to use this gift outside the walls of the church. When you are out doing your daily routine, pray that God will give you a message for people you come in contact with. If He highlights someone to you, be bold and share what He wants you to say. When you share a word from the Lord to someone in the marketplace, it can literally change a life. The key is being confident that it is indeed a message from the Lord and to not let your doubts stop you. God placed on my friend's heart the need to take her children to church. One day, while she was running errands, she was approached by a stranger who said "God wants you to find a church." This statement confirmed what my friend was already feeling and it was what she needed to take the next step. Whatever God is telling you to share, no matter how simple it seems to be–be obedient and share it.

SERVING: A willingness to serve in any capacity whether that be at church, work, or for the community; you find fulfillment in helping others regardless of recognition; you have a servant's heart–just like Jesus.

Ideas: Your gift really is the desire to serve in just about any area needed. You serve the best when you use your skills and talents. If you are good at organizing, serve in any way that involves organization or planning. If you love kids, serve in the children's ministry at church. If you have a heart for the elderly, find opportunities in your community to serve at a retirement home. Whatever you are good at and have a passion for will be the best fit for your serving gift. Also, look for opportunities to serve those in your community who need help but won't ask. The fact that you even offer your services is a great witnessing tool, plus it provides opportunities to meet new people.

TEACHING: The ability to naturally communicate your knowledge in any area is your gift; you love to see others learn new things; you find great satisfaction in sharing your knowledge and skill with others; you are very patient in the instructional process.

Ideas: Hopefully you already either work or volunteer as a teacher. Teaching your students is your ministry. Realize that being a teacher for today's kids is a huge outreach opportunity in and of itself. Pray for your class often and be aware of special opportunities to reach out to their families when they have a need. Teaching a Bible study at church or starting one in your home is another good use of your gift. Consider teaching a class on a subject that you are passionate about at church. If you hear about a child who is struggling in school, offer to tutor. If you can, tutor at a discounted fee. Offer to teach one-on-one a new believer's study for someone you know who is searching for the Lord.

WISDOM: God-given awareness of what is wrong and right; many of your friends come to you for advice; you have a wise understanding of biblical truths and know how to apply them to everyday situations; your wisdom is truly a gift from the Lord, not a result of your education or man.

Ideas: People in your life who are going through tough times may seek out your divine wisdom to help them make important decisions. Your wisdom can bring breakthrough in areas where there seems to be confusion. Pray that God gives you the wisdom and right words to say to people who seek your counsel. Also, there may be times when the Holy Spirit will prompt you to approach someone and share God's heart for their situation. This will take boldness, but God will give you the words. Your gift must operate with a heart of compassion that in turn imparts wisdom with love (or it will not be well received.)

WRITING: Naturally expresses or communicates ideas and thoughts into writing; you have the ability to organize concepts and put it in just the right words; you love to see ideas come together on paper; God may have given you a desire to write a message for others in a book or other media.

Ideas: Put life lessons God has taught you into writing. God may want to use your life experiences one day to impact others. Consider self-publishing a book one day with your message. Write notes of encouragement to anyone you know who is going through a stressful time. Start a neighborhood newsletter with encouraging articles, updates on families, and practical tips people would be interested in. This is a great way to get a pulse on the heartbeat of your community. You will always be kept up to date with what is going on in the lives of others in your community and it can provide future opportunities for ministry.

APPENDIX B

Busy Women Who Reached Out

A Willing Servant Steps Out at the Gym

Sometimes God steps in and uses us in ways that can come as a big surprise to us. That's what happened to me.

I belong to a gym and have worked out there for years. You already know the gym is a great place to develop relationships with people that you might not see regularly outside of the gym. In fact, my gym friends and I always laugh whenever we run into each other in real life (where we actually dress up and wear makeup!). Through the years I have become friends with a woman named April. We walk on the treadmill together side by side for 45 minutes to an hour almost every day. As we all know, working out goes by much faster when you have someone to talk to, so we love to talk and share our lives with each other. As I got to know April, I could sense that she was searching for something. I wasn't sure how to approach her about God, so I began talking to her about my activities at church and my family's involvement there. Soon she began sharing with me that she and a friend were visiting churches trying to find that "something."

She shared that they had visited several churches, but she still was not satisfied with her search. I knew the missing link she was searching for was a personal relationship with Jesus Christ. This opened the door to talking to her a bit about Christianity and the different denominations. I began to think of different ways to help my friend. One idea came to me and I asked her if she ever considered attending a Bible study. She said, "No, that's too intimidating." My next idea was to suggest she attend an informative class on Christianity, maybe something similar to a new Christian's class where one could learn about the Bible. Our youngest daughter at that time worked for a Christian organization called Alpha USA. I knew a little about the program and knew that anyone could attend. It was a format where people were free to ask questions of any kind and it sounded like a very welcoming environment for my friend.

I told April about the class and asked if she might want to attend. To my surprise she was very interested! The next step was to find a church that was hosting an Alpha class soon. I called my daughter to help find a class in the area and to my surprise no classes were scheduled at any nearby churches. And to make matters worse, one of the Alpha leaders actually suggested that I do the class in my home for my friend! They said they would send me the videos and all I had to do was show the video and follow the leader's instruction guide. I began to pray, "Lord how can this be happening, you know I am no evangelist, can I really do this?"

I loved my friend, and really wanted her to find what she was looking for and accept Jesus as her Savior. Since I could not get anyone else to step in and lead the class it left no one else but me. I ordered the videos and invited my friend to my home. She said she would come and by the way, was it ok if she brought a friend? Of course I said "Yes." I also thought thanks a lot LORD, now I'm responsible for not only my friend but another person, what if I mess up? A lot of insecurities came into my thoughts, but since I had said "Yes," I had to go through with it. We picked a date and they came to my home. Each week we viewed one video and each week they had the opportunity to accept Jesus. Week after week I didn't see much progress in them accepting the Lord. Finally after viewing about six or so of the videos, April's friend turned to her and said, "Have you prayed and invited Jesus Christ into your life? I have." My friend April and I were both surprised. April said she was not ready yet but was still searching. I am not sure at what point but before the series was over, April also prayed to accept Jesus as her Lord and Savior. It was pretty amazing to realize that these women accepting the Lord did not have much to do with me at all. I just needed to be available and willing to provide the opportunity, God did the rest! You see God was already drawing these women to Him. I really learned a lot, it's not about my ability at all. A great evangelist is not needed, but rather a willing servant. That even I can do.

One Conversation at Work

Often in our busy work days, we do the tasks at hand and forget that each person we work with has a personal life, often with difficult things going on. I remember one day, I was finalizing a report, trying to make an afternoon deadline. A young woman was helping me make all of the final formatting changes. As we worked together, I noticed she seemed stressed and unhappy. I began to pray silently for her and then asked her if everything was okay. She told me that she was robbed the day before. While she was at work, someone had broken into her apartment and stolen many sentimental things that she could not replace. I listened as she shared her story and told her how sorry I was that this had happened.

She cried a little and then thanked me for listening. It was a very simple act, but I saw her countenance change; she was able to share her load and seemed just a little bit lighter as we continued to work!

A Busy Mom Shares God's Love in a Hurry!

It was a typical Sunday-after-church lunch with friends. We were laughing and having a great time at the crowded little hole in the wall Mexican restaurant. As we said good bye to our friends and left the restaurant, I saw a woman out of the corner of my eye. I noticed she sat alone looking hopeless and desperate. As we walked to the car I began talking to the Lord about her. I began asking Him for a specific word of encouragement for her life that would touch her deeply, that way she wouldn't think I was just another religious kook trying to hunt her down. I heard nothing. I said, "Lord, don't You want to tell me something about her so that she will know that You are real and You are God and that You love her?" Nothing. I had heard so many stories in church of God giving people specific, prophetic words about other people as they shared the love of God with them. But I wasn't getting anything. As I was about to get my kids in the car, I saw the woman exit the restaurant and head across the crowded little parking lot to her old car. I knew it was now or never. I told my kids to wait by the car for a minute (they were old enough and I could still see them) while I literally ran across the parking lot to catch this woman before she drove away and my opportunity was missed. I thought that while I might not have a specific word from God for her, I did know that He loved her and died on the cross for her sins and that He could help her. As she was closing her car door, I said, "excuse me, could I talk to you for a minute?" She looked very surprised and a little scared, but she agreed. I said something like this, "I am a Christian and when I was walking by you out of the restaurant, I felt that the Lord wanted me to tell you how much He loves you and cares about you. I was wondering if you need prayer about anything or if you need any help?" The woman began to cry and then to weep. She said, "You know, when I was getting in my car, I looked up to heaven and I said to God, 'Are You really there and do You really care?' and then you showed up at my window." She let me get into her car and she shared some very painful situations she was going through. I gave her my phone number and prayed with her and hugged her good bye. This whole experience happened in less than five minutes. Although I never heard from this precious woman again, I am ever moved by the heart of Jesus for hurting, broken-hearted people and by His desire to let us extend His amazing love to others.

The Church Lady

Usually I work out three times a week at a small fitness place for ladies. The environment is friendly with the exercise equipment located in a circle so we often talk to one another during our workouts. One day, I noticed that one of the ladies, Peggy, was extremely quiet instead of her usual outgoing self. Her eyes were red and swollen and it was obvious that she was upset.

When Peggy got ready to leave, the manager asked me to step outside and talk to Peggy with her. Peggy immediately began to cry uncontrollably and told us that she had just been diagnosed with malignant breast cancer. They planned to do a mastectomy in a couple of days. The manager told Peggy that I was a pastor and asked her if we could pray with her. Peggy shook her head in agreement. I asked Peggy if she believed in the Lord Jesus Christ. She told me that she did. Then I asked her if she believed that the Lord could completely heal her and explained that I was going to pray believing that this would occur. Once again, she responded yes and said she would agree with us in this prayer. We stood outside and prayed and thanked the Lord for making every intricate part of her body. Then we thanked Him for healing her from the top of her head to the bottom of her feet and removing this cancer from her body.

Two weeks later when Peggy went to have her surgery they could not find any cancer. Her doctors were dismayed and perplexed. We thanked the Lord for His answer to prayer and the divine miracle! Peggy told the ladies at the gym what happened and the word quickly spread. Almost immediately, ladies I did not even know asked me if I was the church lady. I began to pray for physical healings: arthritis, ulcers, migraines, high blood pressure, etc.; for relationships to be restored and renewed through the love of the Lord, and for emotional healing for depression, worry, and finances to be restored.

This literally started a ministry for me at my gym where the ladies still refer to me as the "church lady" and continue to ask for prayer. God simply wants us to be willing and available to serve Him. It is not about our ability, but our availability. We have seen ladies healed physically, emotionally, marriages restored supernaturally, and jobs have been provided to meet financial needs. This has opened up the door for me to share about Jesus Christ and His love, and we have ladies who have asked Him into their hearts and are now going to church.

Massage Therapy and God

One of the best Mother's Day gifts my husband ever gave me was a membership for a monthly massage, although I did find it difficult to take the time to indulge myself in this brief luxury.

There were several great gals that I preferred to do my massage. One in particular was a single mother who supported her eight-year-old son. I always enjoyed visiting with her. During one massage, I had just started to unwind when Jenny began to talk about being diagnosed with cervical cancer four days prior. She went on to say that she wasn't afraid and told her doctor to just remove everything. Her doctor thought her comments were too radical and wanted to discuss it further with her. He wanted to run more tests, but she was insistent that she wanted to get a hysterectomy.

As I lay there on my stomach while she worked on my back, I thought to myself, Is this a God moment? Why now? All I wanted to do was relax, but somehow I knew I was there for a reason.

I listened to her talk and encouraged her with some of the things I had gone through. My mind raced for the right things to say and I asked God to show me what to do. Should I pray for her right then and there? Should I just tell her I would pray for her and leave? I decided I would know at the right time what to do since I didn't feel an immediate urgency to do anything.

As my 50 minutes of luxury came to an end, Jenny left the room. As I was dressing, I still wasn't sure what I was going to do. I knew Jenny was on the other side of the door waiting to give me a cup of water and escort me to the exit.

I opened the door to leave and she gave me the cup of water. I said to her, "I will be praying for you." I then stopped myself and looked her straight in the eyes and said, "May I pray for you right now?" She said, "Yes, please do."

We went back into the massage room and I took her hands and began to pray for her healing and peace of mind. When I finished, she grabbed and hugged me. She started to cry and held on to me for a long time. When she broke loose, I told her that she needed to read the book of Psalms in the Bible. I asked her if she had a Bible and she said yes. I suggested she go to the book of James and read chapter 1.

The book of James has always been one that I turn to when facing trials.

I told Jenny that the first chapter talks about perseverance in time of trouble. She let out a small scream. Her eyes were like saucers. She then told me that she had a tattoo on her back that said *Persevere*!

When she told me that, I knew God had spoken and used me to encourage her. Who would ever think that God would use my getting a massage to make a difference in someone else's life?

Waiting for an Invitation

The thought of sharing my faith with anyone has always been scary to me. Rejection and anger was the reaction I always expected, so I told myself it was easier to avoid it. How do you bring up God in casual conversation anyway? After all, I didn't want to push my faith onto anyone or offend anyone.

Recently however, I began playing tennis with a friend I had met at my daughter's school a couple of years ago. She knew I went to church and began to ask me questions one day after our tennis lesson. She shared about growing up in a boarding school in India that had a Christian influence. When she came to America she expected Americans to talk about God and was surprised that American children didn't pray in schools. She explained that she had been in this country for 10 years, but no one has ever really talked with her about God until she met me. We continued to talk for about an hour. The next week we had breakfast together and I invited her to church with me. She and her daughter came the very next Sunday!

APPENDIX C

Your Story through the Eyes of God
(Questionnaire)

On a separate sheet of paper or in your journal answer the following questions. After you are done, take some time to write your story from God's perspective. This can be a great tool in understanding when the gifts and talents in your life were opened and when some of them may have been buried. It is God's desire that you take steps to recognize and use what He has given you to fulfill *the purposes of His heart* for your life now, not when you are less busy.

- ❖ Where and when were you born?

- ❖ Where did you live during the majority of your childhood days?

- ❖ Who were your friends?

- What were you doing in your earliest childhood memory?

- What types of things did you love to play as a child?

- What are you really good at?

- What role playing did you do with your friends? For example, if you played store, were you the clerk or the shopper? Playing school, were you the teacher or the student?

- What types or groups of people do you most have a heart for? (Women, children, elderly, the sick, teenagers, etc.) Who touches your heart the most?

- What are you doing when you feel most fulfilled?

- What do you get the most excited about where you can't sleep at night?

- What would God say your gifts and talents are?

- Why do you think He created you to live in this generation?

- What experiences have you had in life that used some of your gifts and talents?

- Do you feel that you have some untapped gifts that you are fearful of using? Why? What is the worst thing that can happen?

- When did you first realize who God was and that He desired to have a personal relationship with you? Do you remember the moment you made a decision to ask Him into your life as Lord and Savior?

❖ What have you done with your gifts and talents to make Him proud?

APPENDIX D

Resources for Responding to God's Purposes

Outreach:
Conspiracy of Kindness by Steve Sjogren. Ventura, CA: Regal Books, 2003.

How to Talk about Jesus without Freaking Out by Jim & Karen Covell and Victorya Michaels Rogers. Sisters, OR: Multnomah Publishers Inc., 2000.

Just Walk Across the Room by Bill Hybels. Grand Rapids, MI: Zondervan, 2006.

Share Jesus without Fear by William Fay. Nashville, TN: B&H Publishing Group, 1999

Spiritual Development:
A Busy Woman's Guide to Prayer by Cheri Fuller. Brentwood, TN: Integrity Publishers, 2005.

Having a Mary Spirit by Joanna Weaver. Colorado Springs, CO: WaterBrook Press, 2006.

Having a Mary Heart in a Martha World by Joanna Weaver. Colorado Springs, CO: WaterBrook Press, 2002.

Living Out Your Purpose:
Believe that You Can by Jentezen Franklin. Lake Mary, FL: Charisma House, 2008.

Life Management for Busy Women by Elizabeth George. Eugene, OR: Harvest House Publishers, 2002.

Purpose Driven Life by Rick Warren. Grand Rapids, MI: Zondervan, 2002.

NOTES

[1]*Just Walk Across the Room* by Bill Hybels. Grand Rapids, MI: Zondervan, 2006.

[2]Saint Teresa of Avila Prayer

[3]*My Way His Way* by Carol Hopson. Enumclaw, WA: Winepress Publishing, 2002.

[4]The American Heritage® Dictionary of the English Language, Fourth Edition Copyright © 2006 by Houghton Mifflin Company.

[5]Hughes, *Liberating Your Ministry*, 72-3

[6]*Having a Mary Heart in a Martha World* by Joanna Weaver. Colorado Springs, CO: WaterBrook Press, 2002.

[7]*My Heart-Christ's Home: A Story for Young & Old* by Robert Boyd Munger. InterVarsity Press; Gift edition (June 2001)

[8]Dictionary.com. Unabridged (v 1.1). Random House, Inc.

[9]*Freedom from Busyness: Biblical Help for Overloaded People* by Michael Zigarelli. Lifeway Press, 2005.

[10]*Battlefield of the Mind* by Joyce Meyer. FaithWords (October 2002)

[11]*Straight Talk* by James Dobson. Dallas: Word Publishing, 1991.

Some names have been changed in Appendix B to protect the privacy of others.

ABOUT THE AUTHOR

Tiffany Lynn Milby lives in Southern California with her husband Mike, and three active children—Austin, Alexis and Aaron. Tiffany, married 18 years to her high school sweetheart, can be found on the soccer or baseball field most Saturdays cheering for her children. As a busy mom, much of her time is spent driving her children to activities and volunteering at her children's public school. Tiffany is chairperson of the PTA Family Outreach Committee and founded a Cooking Co-op team. She started this group to help families that are experiencing a crisis by delivering them home cooked meals. She is also an evangelist in her community who started *Moms' Christian Fellowship*, a Bible study for moms with school-aged children. She is also a former church outreach director and has planned many community outreach events designed to bring Jesus into the public marketplace. As a result, thousands have been reached with the message of Christ. She has written the evangelistic booklet, "Searching for More" which has been distributed to hundreds of people.

Tiffany is a key-note and workshop speaker available to minister at conferences, retreats and small groups. Her passion is to encourage busy women in this generation to rise up and not let busyness hinder them from fulfilling God's plans and purposes for their lives. She loves to encourage women to be whom God designed them to be which results in lives that naturally demonstrate Christ to others.

To receive more information about scheduling Tiffany to speak at your event or to share a story of your own about reaching out, please contact her at:

Tiffany Lynn Milby
417 Associated Road #265
Brea, CA 92821
714-524-7446
E-mail: info@purposesofhisheart.org

www.purposesofhisheart.org

www.ingramcontent.com/pod-product-compliance
Lightning Source LLC
Chambersburg PA
CBHW051802040426
42446CB00007B/474